"If you think that networking in the 21st century is passing out business cards as fast as you can, or hiding behind a social media profile, this book will set you straight. David combines theory and practice into an approach that anyone from a rookie professional to a veteran executive can use and should!"

Michael J. Muriel
Central Region Manager for Vector Marketing

"In the course of my career, I've found that the technical skills aren't always sufficient of success. Knowing the law is just a part of being a great lawyer; it's the relationships you build that create the means to navigate in the professional world. I've known David for years, and I've watched him apply the tools in Networking in the 21st Century to build his network, and to help the clients he works with. In fact, networking is how we met! If you are ready to build relationships the right way, don't waste time – make this the next book you read!"

Pia Thompson
Executive Director/Deputy General Counsel
Global Management Consulting Firm

"I knew the author in college, and we got back in touch because he very effectively networked with me. And that's what you'll get out of Networking in the 21st Century - tactics that work in the real world of fast-paced information and insanely busy people. David uses a humorous, down-to-earth, and conversational approach to unpack best practices from creating relationships outside your immediate sphere to asking the relevant "next question." I've been in this space for 10 years and I learned a thing or two!"

Ale
*Blind Spots: The 10 Business M
Believe on Y
and They Don't Tec*

"As we get older, time seems to become a scarcer and scarcer resource. Networking in the 21st Century distills the essence of how to build the relationships that you need to succeed in business and in life—a critical path to ensure optimal use of your time."

Adam Stock
Financial Planning Guru and
Founder of The Next Level Planning Group

"If you are in business—and especially if you're in sales—this book will make you way more efficient at meeting the people you need to be successful. For the last seven years, D. Fish has made a study out of understanding how social media changes networking. He has answers to questions like: How do you make a strong first impression when you're being looked up online before a meeting? and How do you find balance when people expect 24/7 accessibility? His answers are direct, easy to follow, and easy to execute."

Jason Seiden, entrepreneur and author of
Super Staying Power: What You Need to
Become Valuable and Resilient at Work

"David Fisher has developed the comprehensive blueprint most books on networking are missing! He helps you to understand the obstacles that have kept you from creating a vibrant network in the past and then shows you how to develop strategies to inform and influence your tactics moving forward. Why re-invent the wheel when you can learn from a master who has used this field-tested approach to become a top producer and successful entrepreneur."

Joey Davenport, CLU, CLF
President of the Hoopis Performance Network

Networking in the 21st Century: Why Your Network Sucks and What You Can Do About It

DAVID J.P. FISHER

A RockStar Publishing Book

Edited by Nancy L. Baumann

Cover Design by Debbie O'Byrne
Interior Design by JETLAUNCH

Library of Congress Control Number:
ISBN: 978-0-9841236-2-9
MOBI ISBN: 978-0-9841236-3-6
EPUB ISBN 978-0-9841236-4-3

Printed in the United States
10 9 8 7 6 5 4 3 2 1

Contents

Introduction 7

Section I: How Your Network Got In the Condition It's In

Chapter 1:   What the $^*@ is networking?! 13
Chapter 2:   But is this really worth my time? 22
Chapter 3:   Why Has Your Networking Sucked? 27
Chapter 4:   Weak is the New Strong 37
Chapter 5:   Are You an Introverted or Extroverted Networker? 47
Chapter 6:   The Social Media 57

Section II: Unsucking Your Networking

Chapter 7:   The Path Forward 69
Chapter 8:   Become an Autodidact 72
Chapter 9:   Become Socially Savvy 79
Chapter 9.5 Personal Development 91
Chapter 10: Make Technology Your Friend 95
Chapter 11: Live a Profersonal™ Life 114

Section III: Taking Steps to Unsuck Your Network!

Let's Talk Tactics! 125
Concluding Thoughts 189

For my parents Mary and John,
my first and best networking teachers

Introduction

What are you trying to accomplish in your professional life right now? What are your goals, your dreams, your aspirations? We each have a vision for the future that we carry in our hearts and minds, but no matter how unique our goals are, we have one thing in common: We need help to accomplish them. We traverse through webs of relationships and connections, and what ultimately determines our professional success is how skillfully we navigate them. If we want to rise to the heights of our fields, develop reputations as skilled and competent experts, and become financially successful, we need help from others.

This book had its birth on February 1, 2006, the day I "officially" started my own professional development firm. I had just finished my ribbon-cutting ceremony, which consisted of a piece of ribbon stretched over the desk in my home office, along with a pizza with two friends. My friends left, and I sat at that desk and thought, "Now what the hell am I going to do?" I had started my own company because I didn't like my other options (I would find out over the next ten years that this is not an uncommon reason), which meant that I hadn't taken time for business planning or to create a marketing system. Even worse, my service offerings were simply a page I'd thrown up on a hastily constructed website.

I needed clients, but I wasn't sure how to get them. I didn't know what kind of marketing would work. Oh, and I didn't have an advertising budget. Not that I hadn't constructed a budget, it's just that the budget wasn't funded because I didn't have any money. So I reviewed a checklist of marketing ideas I'd found online and measured myself against them. I couldn't afford newspaper ads or radio. I didn't have the reputation to do public speaking. Social media wasn't on the scene yet. (Heck, Facebook wouldn't even open up its membership until that September.) I didn't know how to generate enough traffic to make a blogging or pay-per-click campaign work. And I didn't think passing out flyers would sell business coaching and training services.

But the word "networking" kept popping up on the list. Ah, now here was something that held some promise. One thing I could do was go out, meet new people, and talk to them. I'd spent time during college and immediately after as a top direct-sales representative for Cutco Cutlery, selling kitchen cutlery in people's homes. I had risen to sales manager in the Chicago area and ultimately trained over 1,500 new salespeople. I had long ago gotten over my fear of meeting new people, so if there was one thing I felt comfortable with it was talking to people. I knew that if I could call a stranger on the phone, set up an appointment, and then go sell them knives in their own kitchen, I could approach someone at a networking event and give them a business card. I looked up a local networking event—and the rest is history.

Well, not quite. My goal with this book is to minimize your learning curve, because I certainly had a steep one. I want to help you get past the years of trial and error I waded through to build my professional network—and there was a lot of trial and error. I started from square one, and I had to learn what was working and what wasn't at the same time that I was building my network. It wasn't as easy as I thought it would be, but I kept at it. For a while, I became a networking machine. I would go to at least one or two networking events every week, and I had hundreds of networking coffee meetings. I read books and articles about networking and eventually started writing my own. I immersed myself in building connections with as many people as I could.

While doing this, I learned about "networking karma." Experienced networkers know that the more you give to your network, the more good stuff comes back to you. I had an interesting opportunity to give back to my network because I'm a RockStar. I mean, not a real one, but I had played in a band for years and was comfortable in front of a group as a speaker. I used my public speaking experience to emcee the networking events I attended because one, I wanted to give back in a way that would help, and two, like a real rock star, I wasn't a morning person. Because networking events were usually breakfast meetings, being the host ensured that I would get to these events on time. While leading these meetings, I got in the habit of sharing some of the networking tips I was learning with the group so they could get the most out of the experience. Double the networking karma!

That led to more speaking engagements about networking and to working with coaching clients on how to improve their networking. When social media came along, I jumped on LinkedIn as a way to expand my circle and started training people on doing the same. I eventually helped develop the training program at Ajax Workforce Marketing, the only LinkedIn preferred partner for branding and training in North America. As their Director of Training, I helped teach thousands of professionals how to build effective personal brands and relationships online. I also wrote a short handbook on networking called *Step by Step Networking*, and I continued to write articles and make short videos on how to improve as a networker.

But the proof is in the pudding as they say, and I'm most proud of the fact that almost ten years later, I'm still at the same desk—but I no longer ask what I'm supposed to do. I've built a career and a business based on the relationships I created with the thousands of professionals I've met over the years. It didn't happen overnight, but it will happen for you if you focus your efforts on doing the right activities the right way for the right reasons.

It worked for me—let me show you how it can work for you.

Section I

HOW YOUR NETWORK GOT IN THE CONDITION IT'S IN

Chapter 1

What the $^*@ is networking?!

O kay, let's get a dirty little secret out of the way right from the start: There isn't one generally accepted definition of networking. So if you haven't been able to figure out what it is so far, you're in pretty good company. It's a word like "freedom" or "love;" it's pretty much impossible to get everyone to agree on what networking actually is. If you asked ten people to define it, you'd get back eleven answers. That is, if you got back clear answers at all because a lot of people tend to view networking like a certain Judge Potter Stewart defined obscenity: "I know it when I see it." We think we'll know networking when we see it and that we can just point at a conversation and go, "Yep, that's some networking going on over there."

Apparently you'll just know networking when you run into it. And apparently you'll be running into it all the time because it's so important. It seems like everywhere you go for career advice, people tell you that networking is the key to surviving and thriving in our careers. We hear sayings like, "It's not what you know, it's who you know." We read books like Malcolm Gladwell's *The Tipping Point* that talk about Connectors, and we think we have to be one to be successful. We go to our local Big Box of Books retailer or to Amazon's "Here Are the Business Books You MUST Read" and find a long list of titles such as *Networking Like a Pro, Making Connections Count,* and *Networking for People Who Hate Networking* (oh, yeah, and this book). So networking must be really, really important for career success!

But right from the beginning we have a dilemma. We're only two paragraphs into a book on networking, and we already have a basic conflict. Nobody knows exactly what networking is—and yet we're told it's critical for career success. It's ludicrous to think we can build competence and confidence in something that we can't even define. If we don't know what networking is, how the heck are we supposed to improve it? Is anyone really even "networking" in the first place? It's hard to learn a skill when you can't agree on what it is, so one of the reasons why most of us aren't very good at networking is that we actually don't know what we're trying to do. We hope to stumble upon a magic room where everyone is *networking* (cue trumpet sounds for added effect); the clouds will part, and we'll just "get it." Boom! Our career will take off and we'll be massively successful.

> *It's hard to learn a skill when you can't agree on what it is, so one of the reasons why most of us aren't very good at networking is that we actually don't know what we're trying to do.*

What's more likely is the typical path you've probably already experienced. We graduate from school, having learned nothing about professional networking (more on that later) and hopefully stumble into our first job. If we're lucky enough to find a good mentor, we hear, "You should build your network. That's how you get ahead." Okay, sounds reasonable. As we start our careers, we dive into building our network—or we think we're networking because we go to events and activities that have "networking" in the title. We go to *networking* breakfasts and *networking* cocktail receptions and *networking* alumni get-togethers. We do it in good faith, thinking that if we keep showing up, something good will happen. We keep waiting for the benefits of our efforts—you know, all the great introductions and referrals and job opportunities and professional development that's supposed to come ... and we keep waiting.

And we keep waiting.

And we keep waiting.

Eventually, even though we're still waiting, our time at work is spent knee-deep in projects, meetings, and emails, and our personal life is consumed with things like mortgages and families. We don't have time to keep going to things that have "networking" in the title. We start to feel the time squeeze, and something has to give. Since we've rarely seen or can't remember the direct benefits of all our networking, we just say, "Screw it" and relegate professional networking to the same place as world peace or saving the environment. Great concepts but not that practical—and definitely not something we have time to do.

I wish this was an uncommon story, but I've met enough professionals to know that this scenario has been repeated innumerable times, and it's the reason professional networking gets such a bum rap. It's a nasty, unproductive cycle. We don't know what networking is or how to do it, and then we feel awful when we aren't successful—which short-circuits any further attempt to further our careers through networking. Rinse and repeat.

So what do you do?

First of all, let's breathe a little. Bring it down a bit. I promise it's going to be all good. Let me get you some chamomile tea. Feeling a little better? Great.

We're going to talk about networking in this book. What it is, why you've struggled with it, how to get better at it—the whole nine yards. We'll start with the knowledge that you already have all the tools you need. You just have to put them together the right way. Sure, we're going to get intentional and focus on ways to strengthen your competence and confidence, but you already know how to build a network. If you have built a relationship with at least one other person up to this point in your life, you already have the foundation for success. In fact, unless you live alone in a cave, you have a network already in place. You just don't pay attention to it because you're always surrounded by it.

> *If you have built a relationship with at least one other person up to this point in your life, you already have the foundation for success.*

It's like asking a fish about water. They don't even realize it's there because it's always there. Your friends, co-workers, family, colleagues, old classmates, neighbors ... they are a network—they are *your* network. We are social creatures, and it's completely natural for us to be in a web of relationships. In fact, through those very relationships, we found our jobs, our significant others—even tips on new bands to get hip to. There's a good chance you've already received the benefits of networking; it's just been completely accidental most of the time, so you may not have recognized it. Instead of thinking that *networking works*, we assume it's something that happens here and there when the people we already know help us out.

It's important to bring some focus and some deliberateness to our networking to make it a more useful part of our lives—especially in our professional spheres. Unfortunately, most of us tend to associate being deliberate with being obnoxious or aggressive. We think that we have to accumulate a huge group of connections by introducing ourselves to every person we meet. This turns us off from networking because most of us have the stereotype of the over-the-top salesperson in mind, the one who goes to an event and tries to meet (and sell) everyone in the room. Their obnoxiousness causes most of us well-meaning individuals to stay away from that behavior. We don't want to be that person!

That's unfortunate because these overly assertive people have the right intentions, but the wrong execution. They might not be skillful or subtle, but that business-card-passing-out machine at your local Chamber of Commerce meeting is doing something right. At least he or she is purposefully going out to meet new connections. They are trying to increase the size of their network, which in theory (a correct one, which we'll see later) will help them accomplish their business goals. But why does it still feel "off" to most of us?

Perhaps we realize that at some level, networking actually has a selling component to it. And for many of us, "sales" is a four-letter word connected to an image of a used-car salesman on the hustle. We won't do that to other people and don't want to be perceived as slimy, so we stay away from selling. But when networking is done right, it's about representing the one thing that we should all feel confident in: Ourselves! We don't want to push ourselves on others, but we do want to find a middle ground where we can advocate for ourselves and our careers without being seen as high-pressure or annoying.

> *When networking is done right, it's about representing the one thing that we should all feel confident in: Ourselves!*

In the case of the over-the-top, aggressive networker, they often miss the mark when it comes to the key elements of relationship building. For example, they might fail to notice social cues or push their agenda too much. They miss the opportunity to create a mutual relationship, one that is balanced. On an intuitive level, most of us grasp that networking and successful relationship building is based on give and take. This isn't a contest to see how many people we can meet, but an exercise to build a mutually meaningful interaction between two people. Finding support and help *for ourselves* is the reason that most of us start networking, and there's nothing wrong with that. But most of us intuitively understand there should be a reciprocal nature in the relationships and that we should also network *for others*. That's something we learn early on in the nest of our early personal network. We figure out pretty quickly that when we're nice to other people, they're nice back.

To truly see the benefits of this process, we need to move beyond the simple accumulation of names in a database (sorry if you have been hoarding "friends" on Facebook), to building relationships with our connections. It doesn't mean that you have to be best friends with everyone that you come across, but it does mean that you have to use the same social skills you used in grade school to make new friends. Find out what their interests are, what makes them tick, what problems they are trying to solve. On the spectrum between complete stranger and BFF, networking relationships should probably lie a little to the right side of the midline.

Can we simply define networking as cultivating a big handful of relationships? Not quite. Relationships are necessary, but they aren't sufficient. That's why having a bunch of friends doesn't mean that you are a good networker. This brings us to the biggest difference between a professional network and the relationships that you've built up to this point, one that is a key ingredient to you being successful. The basic premise of networking is that there is a purpose to these interactions—to give and receive help. It's not just about knowing people. We build our network to help find new jobs, to get promotions, to find sales leads, etc. We want to create opportunities, and part of that means going to our network to ask for help.

So in putting this all together, we can see that networking includes the following:

1. Having a large number of connections, or at least a number beyond our inner circle of close friends and family
2. Cultivating relationships with our connections that go deeper than simply collecting names and email addresses
3. Having a purpose for those relationships that's usually business related and revolves around creating mutual opportunities

I'm not going to say that I have the perfect definition of what networking is or what it should be, but this is the starting point. More importantly, I want you to have an idea you can grasp, something that allows you to focus your efforts. Let's escape the trap of trying to execute something we can't even define. As a working definition, let's use this:

> *Networking is building a web of relationships with others for mutual support in finding business solutions.*

This definition brings a few important components together that bear mentioning again. Here are the foundational components of a thriving network:

1. Size

The perfect size of an effective professional network can vary, and we'll see that there isn't a perfect size to try to achieve. But we all intuitively understand that it's important to have a network that consists of more than just two or three people. Networking revolves around meeting many new people and bringing them into our sphere of influence.

2. Relationships

When we talk about relationships, we mean going beyond simply connecting a name with a face. There are two important parts to relationship building that will affect how we approach our networking. The first is that there has to be some degree of interpersonal exchange between you and the people in your network. It doesn't mean that you have to be intimate confidants with everyone, but when we think of relationships, we think of people who we know something about and who know something about us. This leads to the second ingredient of a relationship: that it occurs over time. It's not an interaction that happens once and never repeats.

3. Giving

Inherent in these relationships is the idea that you mutually support one another. Many popular networking groups use the mottos "Givers Gain" or "Give to Get" to emphasize the need to be a contributor in your networking relationships. If you're only on the lookout to help yourself, you aren't networking—you're a leech.

4. Seeking Help

It's important to find ways to support the people in your network, but it's also appropriate to seek help for yourself. One of the biggest differences between your natural network and the professional network is that you deliberately ask for help. It's the difference between "hanging out" with someone and actually networking. It doesn't mean we don't get help from our natural networks of friends, family, and neighbors. We actually get a lot of support from our personal relationships, but it tends to be an afterthought and accidental. The purpose of the business network is to help everyone in it be more successful. Just like you help them, you too can ask for help. It means that you should be looking for support just as you are giving it.

Great, now we know what networking is—but what do we do with that? Now that you know what networking is, maybe you aren't inspired and you want to go read something else. You could do that, but you'd be missing out because the definition is the smallest piece of the puzzle—and not one of the sexiest parts. I mean, a definition isn't going to help you get a new job, right? But it does give you a clue about what comes next; it puts you on the right path. If we can't conceptualize it, we can't do it. So let's start walking the path, and let me show you why spending time developing your network is a very good idea.

Chapter 2

But is this really worth my time?

Now that we have a much better idea of what networking is, we have to ask the question: Is it really worth my time? I mean, relationships are good, and having people help you with your career is good, but we are all so busy! Between the 97 emails you have to answer, the 6 meetings on today's calendar, and your lunchtime yoga class, do you really have time to create a strong network?

The answer that most people give is a resounding, "No!" Actually, it's not really a resounding "no," but more of a loud sigh punctuated with tiredness and defeat. One of the most common objections I hear is that networking takes too much time, too much attention, and requires too much darn energy. We think that networking will steal the few scant moments left in our already overstuffed schedules, so why bother? We're right about one thing: Networking *does* take time and energy. But (and there is a but!), it takes a lot less effort than we think if we do it right. If you're one of those professionals who think that putting *any* effort into building your network is daunting, then keep reading.

I once worked with a client who was a successful attorney in downtown Chicago. She was stuck. She knew that she needed to network to find clients, but didn't think she had time. She wanted to move up, and saw that the partners who were rainmakers—who brought in new clients—were the ones who got the nod. So she went to professional events and met contacts for lunch, but then she would fall behind on her billable client work and have to scramble to catch up. That, in turn, left a bunch of follow-up emails from her networking connections sitting in her inbox, all unanswered. When she got caught up on her work, she'd try to get back in touch with them—and the cycle would repeat. She was tired and frustrated because it seemed like there was no way out of the time trap for her. She couldn't figure out how to balance her immediate responsibilities with her long-term goals. Sound familiar?

Most of us see the downsides of networking (time, energy, substandard appetizers at networking events), but we fail to see the upside. And this tremendous upside can get overlooked because the relationship between the input and the outcome is often hard to measure. The positive results of our efforts aren't usually immediate or obvious, and most people want to see a straight path between networking time and the payoff before they commit. They want to see an obvious and immediate return on investment (ROI), which is the only way they'll know if the appointment or event was a valuable use of their time. They don't have time to figure out if it was worth it or not.

> *This tremendous upside can get overlooked because the relationship between the input and the outcome is often hard to measure.*

So the average professional gets caught in a downward spiral. Since the benefits aren't immediately apparent, networking becomes an increasingly frustrating endeavor. When people get frustrated, they start "phoning it in." They don't put a lot of effort into their networking, but if you ask them, they still think they do. Subconsciously, they take more and more shortcuts and, even when they're in a networking situation, put little emotional focus into it. And if their "checked out" status isn't obvious to them, it certainly is to the people they're with. Thus, they get even less benefit than before, which seems to prove what they thought all along—that networking is a waste of time. So they put even less focus on it and end up like a lot of professionals: stuck in their career with few connections or new opportunities. And when someone comes along and tells them they should network, they snarl and say, "I tried that, and it doesn't work." Their networks suck, and they think it's networking's fault.

This is where our definition of networking can swoop down and save us. When we defined networking, we saw that networking isn't a simple "set it and forget it" process. It doesn't work that way. There's rarely a direct correlation between a networking activity and a result from it. For example, I often get invited to emcee networking meetings for associations and organizations, and I often say that "no one ever writes a contract at a networking event." Of course, there's always one smart aleck in the group who pipes up and says they once sold Girl Scout cookies or something. But this kind of comment actually proves the point because most of us aim for something much more long-term than selling a box of cookies.

> *There's rarely a direct correlation between a networking activity and a result from it.*

The networking process is actually quite shapeless, and that can throw us off the trail. If you think the benefits should come immediately after the activity, you're setting yourself up for failure. Actually, to be precise, networking does have a form, a structure; but it's definitely not linear. It's more like an amorphous cloud. As you inject energy into this cloud, you increase the likelihood that opportunities will emerge. They might show up quickly—you connect with someone and find out they have a hot career tip you can work on right away. Or the benefit might show up later—you build a relationship with someone over the years, and then one day they get a promotion and hire you for a project.

We foolishly think networking looks like this:

Meet someone → Have a conversation → Advance your career

In reality, it probably looks more like this:

Meet someone → Meet them again → Send follow-up email → Meet someone else that knows them → Grab lunch together → Send them a follow-up email → Introduce them to someone who can help with their career → Stay in touch for six months with occasional email → Have a phone conversation → Get introduced to someone who can help → Advance your career

Even though it's not always obvious, the benefits of cultivating a strong network do exist. I bet you can think of examples where your relationships have been important sources of information and opportunity. How often do people find jobs or significant others through someone they know? Whether the person who sits next to you on the plane tells you about a job lead, or your friend introduces you to her friend from college (who eventually becomes your wife), again and again we hear stories where the network comes through. And these happenstance encounters and conversations tease us. It's almost as if these accidental successes show us what could be, but we don't know how to make them happen on purpose.

Dating is an easy place to see the benefits of networking—and the pitfalls. It's actually a given that most people find their mates through the network effect, whether it's through friends of friends or spending time in social groups where everyone has shared interests. You even have professional connectors (matchmakers) who facilitate these interactions. But you never know what activity is going to lead to what results. It's why they say "you'll find someone when you aren't looking." It's not that you aren't looking; it's that there are so many variables that you don't recognize the critical ones as they happen. How were you supposed to know that going to a specific party with a specific friend—who introduced you to her college roommate's friend—would lead you to marital bliss?

And that's what frustrates most people. Sometimes it works. Sometimes it doesn't. The effort we put in seems to give nothing back. And then someone from our past calls with the perfect job opportunity. So it kinda works, and it kinda doesn't. How can we escape the cycle of wasted time and effort and hone in on what's most important? And if there's so much uncertainty, does it make sense to prioritize networking as part of your business life?

In short, yes it does.

Chapter 3

Why Has Your Networking Sucked?

Now that you know there are benefits to networking, you can just put this book down, go build a network that will rival the empires of old, and your career will be the envy of millions. Or maybe that's jumping the gun a bit. Before you picked up this book, you probably understood the value of networking (at least a little), or you wouldn't have started reading at all. Everyone seems to be interested in getting advice on how to build a more powerful network.

So why do so many professionals struggle with networking? And more to the point, why do so many struggle to get any business benefit from it? There are two aspects to the process that you must wrap your head around. First we have to build the network. We have to connect with other professionals, and then build relationships with them over time. Then we have to translate them into useful career help. You can have great relationships with other professionals, but that doesn't matter if you can't leverage those relationships to further your career. We have to create the connections and then we have to get valuable help from them. Most of us struggle with one or the other, and often both. So what's the problem? Is it that some of us are hopelessly socially awkward? Maybe. Is it that the majority of us don't know what we're doing? Probably.

Networking requires a careful balance of interpersonal skills and professional acumen to be successful. Unfortunately, no matter how good we think we are, we all start behind the eight-ball when it comes to business relationships. And it's not our fault! When we look at the science of human relationships and the history of how humans interact, we see that in many ways humans are predisposed to be really bad at professional networking. As you are meeting people, passing out business cards and having lunch appointments, you are actually fighting against hundreds of thousands of years of human evolution. This, as you might imagine, can make things pretty tough.

At first blush this may sound pretty dire, but as we'll see later, there is hope. But if we're going to move past these obstacles, we have to first understand the challenges. I promise this won't turn into a boring college lecture, but if we want to get past our challenges, we have to look at how humans are wired to interact with each other. In other words, knowing why your network sucks in the first place is half the battle.

Let's start at the beginning. We take for granted that we interact and build relationships, but that isn't necessarily a given. Why do we have networks in the first place? Why aren't we solitary animals like bears or tigers? The answer is simple: we're actually wired to be social creatures. Over hundreds of thousands of years, humans have developed the mental skills (and big brains) necessary to gather into groups for protection and support. Things like speech, imagination, and even empathy are all wonderful adaptations when you are cooperating with a group instead of living on your own. Being in a group meant it was easier to gather food, to raise our young, and to protect ourselves from marauding carnivores. We became much more like the pack-living wolves than the bears or jungle cats that prowled around by themselves.

If you think about it, those elements of the human experience are also a requirement for professional networking. If people, by nature, were uncommunicative, unhelpful, and loners—well, networking would be tough. Humans developed communication skills like speech and facial expressions to interact with each other. We developed nuanced emotional responses to mitigate stress and found the value in forming powerful bonds between each other. There's even evidence that qualities like generosity and truthfulness are driven by evolutionary pressures to get along.

Over huge stretches of time, we got better and better at working together. We got good at building interpersonal relationships. We organized ourselves into groups and structures, like families, tribes, and clans. We spread around the globe, which allowed for (and necessitated) further sophistication of our social abilities. The human brain continued to develop, and humans continued to refine their intricate and complex social skills to allow for more and more effective cooperation.

Most of this development was in a very specific social environment, one that is much different than where we find ourselves today. For thousands and thousands of years, we lived in small hunter-gatherer groups. Some would consist of just a few families, and others were larger clans, but there was a logistical upper limit. The group had to be agile enough to move to new food sources when they exhausted their current supplies. You still see this behavior in aboriginal cultures in South America, Africa, and Australia. In fact, historians and anthropologists think we didn't start living in true cities (and thus larger groups) until maybe 10,000 BCE—which is barely a blink on the human timeline.

So all of our communication skills were developed to build stronger relationships, but they were nurtured in very different circumstances than today. In most cases, we would have known everyone in our social sphere; in fact, we probably would have been related. It would have been rare to run into someone new. That's hard for us to realize in a time when we meet new people on an almost daily basis, and it's not uncommon to have 500+ LinkedIn connections. Compared to today, the world where humans evolved looks very insular and small. But that's where we developed our social skills.

> *All of our communication skills were developed to build stronger relationships, but they were nurtured in very different circumstances than today.*

The distinction between then and now is important, and it helps us understand why it's hard for us to build a big network. Specifically, it tells us why we're great at starting relationships but terrible at maintaining a lot of them. Anthropologist Robin Dunbar examined this problem and noted that the size of primate groups changed, depending on the size of their brains. He wondered if there was a similar correlation regarding how many relationships humans could manage. From his research, he extrapolated what's known as Dunbar's Number, which was later validated by historical analysis of the size of human communities. Dunbar's Number represents the highest number of relationships the average person can manage at one time. It is how many friends and family members we can keep up with at any given time, and it's based on how our brains are wired. And it's not as large a number as you might think—it's only 148. People often round it up to 150 because it's easier to remember, but on average, that's how many relationships we can maintain. Even if you're a relationship genius, one standard deviation from the average Joe only boosts you up to 200—so are you really connected to as many people as you think you are?

You might say, "But I know hundreds and hundreds of people, way more than 150!" And in some ways you're right. You have easily *met* more than 150 in your life; heck, my high school class had 220 people alone. But do you *know* them? You may or may not be able to remember many of their names anymore. Try writing down the names of everyone you know, and I bet you'll be surprised at how hard it is if you can't reference your phonebook or cellphone contacts. Because we are exposed to so many people in our lives, we are *familiar* with many people. But do you really have strong, interpersonal connections with all of them? Probably not. If you look at the list of people you've met in your life, you'll probably realize that you currently have relationships with, well, about 150 of them.

In fact, to form new relationships, we have to let go of existing ones. It may feel odd to think about the process of ending relationships to form new ones, but we do it all of the time. Just think back to your high school days. When you were in high school, you had rich and dynamic relationships with many of your classmates. But after graduation, many of those relationships got lumped together in a mental category called "high school friend." It's as if you only have so many buckets to store relationships in, and when they have filled up, you have to empty one to start a new relationship. It's why reunions are fun—we haven't thought about many of these people in years.

One of the best modern examinations of this idea is Malcolm Gladwell's *The Tipping Point*. He captures different scenarios where this upper limit of relationships has real world effects. From the size of early human settlements to modern day corporations and military units, our ability to manage 150 relationships—but no more—often has unnoticed effects on how we organize ourselves. Even before Robin Dunbar's research, people realized that a group with more than 150 people couldn't rely on the interpersonal relationships of its members for stability. So they either needed to keep groups below this number—by splitting off new tribes or factories, for example—or develop rules and policies to govern larger groups, such as in a military hierarchy and bureaucracy.

Unfortunately for our networking efforts, the evolutionary process that made us good at building relationships also made us bad at forming a large number of them. Even if think you are a relationship superstar, and you can handle twice the average number, that only leaves you with 300 connections. And to give you a glimpse a few chapters down the road, 300 connections probably isn't enough (and few of us are superstars anyway). The truth is, the more relationships you have, the more likely your network will be productive.

> *Unfortunately for our networking efforts, the evolutionary process that made us good at building relationships also made us bad at forming a large number of them.*

So the actual construction of our brain is working against us. Our skills developed in an environment that didn't require many connections. Sure, we needed to create strong bonds between everyone in our village, but that's a lot different than walking into a hotel ballroom for your industry's "Annual Networking Cocktail Hour." How we interact professionally and the value of building a business network is a relatively new idea. When you look at the history, business networking is the new kid on the block, so it makes sense that we haven't mastered it.

By the way, we're talking about Western or American-style networking. How we network and how we interact with others professionally is driven by the society we inhabit. In fact, different cultures require different approaches. Building a network in India is much different than building a network in Indiana. If you connect with people on a global scale, there will be other etiquette and social rules to learn. Be sure to follow their cultural norms when you engage with professionals in different environments. That being said, because we operate in a global economy, many of the bigger cultural differences in business have started to fade. Global connections have led to a global standard of conduct. And because of the predominance of American business, there is definitely a predilection for American-style networking.

It's a relatively new idea that relationships are vital to our economic success. Think back to those small hunter-gatherer tribes of less than 150. If you lived in that environment, the thought of networking is pretty comical because there's no benefit to it. Everyone already knew everyone else, and they were probably related. Also, networking wasn't really necessary because everyone pretty much had the same job: find food, raise the next generation, and keep away the beasties that wanted to eat you.

If we consider the professional life of Bob the Hunter-Gatherer, it looks pretty simple. Bob lived in a small, wandering tribe. He got up in the morning, went hunting with the other members of his tribe, picked some wild fruits and vegetables, and then hung around the fire at night. He did the same thing the next day and the next. In fact, he wouldn't even see other people unless they encountered another tribe, which would probably lead to either a fight or intermarriage... or maybe both.

How things have changed! Now we have Bob the Accountant. This Bob is likely to live in a town or city with far more than 150 people. (There are more than 150 people on my block.) He's surrounded by strangers, and every day he meets more of them. They might be the barista at the corner coffee shop, a new neighbor, or someone he meets at a cocktail reception. Bob can specialize in his work because when there are more people, not everyone has to do the same thing. Bob can be an accountant and play around with numbers on computer screens because he doesn't have to grow his own food, make his own clothes, or build his own house.

When he does meet someone new, there's little chance that he will start a war or try to marry them—which is good because he meets new people on an almost daily basis, and that could get messy. But what he can do is work with them. They could be a potential client or business partner. It could be a salesperson who sells him a piece of accounting software. Rather than having an insular and closed-off life like the ancient Bob, this Bob is constantly exposed to new relationships and new opportunities. And he's only an accountant; imagine the life of that accounting-software salesperson who meets hundreds or even thousands of new people every year!

These two Bobs wouldn't recognize each other's lives. And that's a lot of change in a relatively short amount of time. We don't recognize this because of something called *historicity*—we think the world has always been and will always be pretty much like it is today. Bob the Accountant can only see what the world looks like to him at this stage, just like you can only see how the world looks to you. It also means that we haven't experienced the huge changes in social, economic, and political structures that make the relationships we have important. We have job specialization, social mobility, and cities with millions of people. We were in those hunter-gatherer bands for hundreds of thousands of years, but we have built cities for less than 10,000. There are now over 250 cities with a population of over a million people in the world (my home of Chicago is one of them), but the first one didn't appear until the 2nd century BCE (Rome gets the prize for that one). So this world is actually very new to us.

Over time, new technology and new ideas have chipped away at the rigid social structures that prevented individual progress. For example, in Western Europe you had world-changers like the printing press and the Renaissance. These led to various political and social revolutions in thought and organization. Then there was the huge economic disruption caused by the Industrial Revolution. And it just kept going. This is a gross oversimplification, but let's compress the lessons of hundreds of years of history: New ways to communicate, new ideas about how to organize politically, and new ways to make money all pushed societies to reorganize.

In fact, let's say that Bob the Accountant lives in Chicago near me. He has the benefit of working in a society where he can start and end relationships with new people whenever he wants, where he can take advantage of social mobility that says if he works hard, he can move up economically. It's a vibrant environment where the sum of the whole is greater than the parts. There are a lot of benefits to being a professional in America, but these cultural innovations are only about 200 years old. This is why the here and now—a world connected by intricate webs of communication and knowledge—provides the perfect petri dish for building a network. This couldn't have happened a thousand years ago, and it probably couldn't have happened even a hundred years ago. We love hearing the rags-to-riches stories of Andrew Carnegie, Abraham Lincoln, Oprah Winfrey, Elon Musk, etc. because they show the power of our interconnected world – and they become more common the closer we get to our current day.

We've come a long way from the small nomadic tribes that followed herds of wild beasts. When we look at the journey from then to now, you might conclude that we've arrived at the perfect time to build a network. And you would be right, but we have one small problem: Our biology and physiology haven't yet caught up. When you look at all the advances we've made, it's easy to forget that for hundreds of thousands of years, we lived in those tiny bands of 150 people who lived as hunter-gatherers. The history of our modern civilization is only about 5,000 years old. And our current economic structures have been around less than 300 years.

Hundreds of thousands of years of biology versus 300 years of political and social organization. Which do you think is stronger?

Of course we have problems networking! Our current social structures are a recent addition to the human experience that is thousands and thousands of years old. The social dynamics and rules that govern our advancement in today's world are only a thin veneer that masks a brain designed for a very different world. This, in turn, causes an inner conflict that is frustrating and keeps us from trying to build an effective network because we don't realize why we're struggling. It's amazing how ingrained Dunbar's Number is in our social organization. And what's worse, this upper limit on the number of relationships is a bigger problem than we think. In fact, when you learn about job searches and why the people you barely know are the most important part of your network, you'll find out why your network really sucks. You'll also see that there's a light at the end of the tunnel.

Chapter 4

Weak is the New Strong

With over 23,000 academic citations, it's one of the most-cited papers in sociology, and in those circles, that's like winning the Super Bowl and being inducted into the Hall of Fame and being voted prom queen all at once. Published in 1973, *The Strength of Weak Ties* by Mark Granovetter put forth what seems like a pretty obvious claim to us today: People find jobs through the recommendations of people they know. Based on what we've said about our networks so far, and considering we're all naturally embedded in some form of network from the get-go, it seems obvious.

But Granovetter observed a wrinkle in this referral process that no one else had noticed. Opportunities weren't coming from where you think they would. It wasn't family and close friends that were facilitating introductions; instead, they came from people that were only mildly connected—what Granovetter labeled a "weak connection." This discovery shows how the traditional ideas of networking led to haphazard results, and how we can escape the roadblocks that history and science have set for our networking efforts.

The stereotypical idea of getting a job through your network is pretty simple. Someone you know well—a good friend, a relative, a neighbor—connects you with a job. For example, your parent might recommend you for a job with one of their cousins, or your best friend might find you a position at their workplace. It was assumed that the people who knew you best would be the most motivated to help you. They had the strongest desire to use their connections to help you find opportunities. And since they saw you often, there would be plenty of opportunities to pass that information along.

While Granovetter found that it was indeed common for people to find jobs through people they know, he found that this tended to happen among people who didn't have close ties. So the picture that we had in our heads was wrong. As he writes:

> *"I have used the following categories for frequency of contact: often = at least twice a week; occasionally = more than once a year but less than twice a week; rarely = once a year or less. Of those finding a job through contacts, 16.7% reported they saw their contact often at the time, 55.6% said occasionally, and 27.8% rarely (n=54). The skew is clearly to the weak end of the continuum, suggesting the primacy of structure over motivation."*

Only 16.7% of the opportunities came through people we saw frequently. The last sentence, where he talks about the importance of structure over motivation, is the key to understanding why networking is such a struggle for so many of us. It also shows the way to make it more effective—but more on that later. We have a mental picture of an ideal network full of those with whom we have deep and tight relationships. We think that the people we know very well will be the ones to help us the most. They have the strongest ties to us, and they want to see us succeed, so they will put forth the effort to give us the recommendations, pass on referrals, and make introductions.

But here's the rub: The problem with effective networking isn't one of desire, it's one of ability. Or rather, it's a question of access to information. The better that we know someone, the more likely they are to be in the same circle of information as we are. Think about your best friends, your close family members, your co-workers, or your spouse. They tend to be very similar to you. They read similar blogs, watch similar movies, and go to similar restaurants. Basically, they swim in the same social pools as you, and because of that, they have access to the same sources of information as you.

> *The problem with effective networking isn't one of desire, it's one of ability.*

We see this in the way that online information goes viral. Think of the jokes, memes, and crazy cat videos you've seen on social sites like Facebook. My guess is that you receive these from online friends you don't know very well. Or if you did receive it from someone close to you, they got it from someone on the fringes of their network. These weak connections act as bridges between tightly wound networks. It's how information leaps from one group to another. This is how word-of-mouth advertising works, especially for things like bands, movies, and restaurants. It often takes bumping into someone you don't normally see to learn about the new places you should check out.

> *These weak connections act as bridges between tightly wound networks.*

That's why Granovetter addresses the importance of structure. It's not so much the strength of the relationship that drives the effectiveness of networking, but rather the type of connection. The true power of networking comes from having someone introduce us to a new person or opportunity, someone who lies outside the boundaries of our existing relationships. It's important that they have time away from you to find information that is new and valuable to you.

Granovetter labeled someone you saw at least once a year but less than twice a week a "weak connection." And these weak connections, ironically, are what make a network strong. Having a large structure of weak connections is important because they have access and knowledge we just don't have. In this scenario, it's not our best friend that gets us a new job, but someone we see infrequently—maybe a friend from college or a past workplace that we see every so often.

One of my first jobs in high school was scooping ice cream at Milwaukee's Summerfest. How did I get the job? Well, I hadn't fully developed my own network yet, so it came through my dad's network. The owner of the ice cream stand was the wife of one of my father's old co-workers, with whom he grabbed lunch every couple of months. After one of those lunches, he came home with a job for me. (I think he just wanted me to start paying for my own pizza.) It was one of his weak connections that linked me to my new job.

Based on Granovetter's findings, the goal of successful networking relationships may seem counterintuitive to many of us. In our personal lives, we seek to develop strong, intimate relationships. By extension, we think we should focus on creating strong relationships in all the facets of our lives. But having a lot of weak connections in our professional network is actually more useful because those weak connections have access to new information, which is the key to a robust and valuable network. The more of these relationships you cultivate, the more likely you are to receive a crucial introduction or recommendation that can boost your career.

> *Having a lot of weak connections in our professional network is actually more useful because those weak connections have access to new information, which is the key to a robust and valuable network.*

People often ask me about the ROI, the return on investment, of my own networking. When I look at the sometimes tangled web of connections that lead to new business, it's clear that weak connections are critical. For example, over the years I've had the opportunity to speak on professional development topics for the alumni at Northwestern University, my alma mater. And that is definitely an opportunity brought about by weak connections.

It started almost ten years ago when I ran a development program for the Young Professionals of Evanston, where I live. Someone in the audience worked for the Alumni Association at Northwestern and introduced me to her boss, the director of the entire association. She asked me to speak for a staff in-service day. I met Aspasia Apostolakis (still one of my favorite names of all time), another director there who stayed in touch and came to one of the first LinkedIn training seminars I ran. She asked me to give a webinar about LinkedIn for the Northwestern alumni, and we put together a program that was eventually attended by over 3,500 alumni. I now count Aspasia as a close friend, but back in the beginning she was the epitome of a weak connection, as I would only be in touch with her a couple of times a year.

This is why the size of your network matters. The bigger it is, the more weak connections you have and the more bridges to outside information exist within it. In fact, there's a principle called Metcalfe's Law that speaks to the benefit of growing a network with a large number of connections. Metcalfe's Law states that the value of a network is proportional to the square of the number of connected users of the system (n^2). (Don't worry, I'm not a math person, either.) In simple terms, it means that the more people in the network and the more connections between the people in that network, the more valuable the network is to everyone involved. Think about it, the first person to get a fax machine didn't get any benefit until the second person bought one. And once everyone had one, it was incredibly useful. In the same way, the more connections we have, even if they are weak connections, the more value the network has in general, and the more value for us, specifically.

But we have a handicap. There's that cap on the number of relationships we can manage at a time that Dunbar described. We have an upper limit that prevents us from creating, or more importantly, maintaining, hundreds of weak connections. It would be ideal if we had a Rolodex in our minds, but it doesn't work that way.

Of course your networking hasn't been successful—it can't be. There is a fundamental tension between the two forces. Success comes from high numbers of weak connections, but your brain fizzles out once it hits its upper limit. The few people we hear about that are really successful tend to be outliers who can either freakishly manage many more relationships or (more likely) who have created systems that allow them to do so. Every super-connector that I've ever met uses some kind of system to augment their natural brainpower. They have to, in order to get past their natural limits. We can learn something from their example, but we'll see there are easier ways to do this. (Hint: It's in the next section.) If you don't have a workable system, you are destined to fail.

This is why you've felt pushed to build your network but have failed to do so. To get the most benefit from networking you need two things. First, you need a way to bring a large group of weak connections into your network. For some people, that isn't too hard; they might have a job like sales or recruiting where they interact with a lot of new people on a regular basis. Or maybe they have a personality that is naturally gregarious, which enables them to make connections in their daily lives—at the grocery store, at church, at their kids' soccer games.

But what if you didn't have that kind of job? What if your daily life is populated by pretty much the same people day in and day out? Or what if you don't have a natural proclivity to start a conversation with the person on the elevator? You struggle because you aren't adding enough people to your network. And if adding new people to your network creates new nodes of information, the flip side is a stagnant network devoid of new information. In this case, you are pretty much stuck knowing the same stuff as everyone around you.

Secondly, even if you can bring lots of fresh connections to your business life, you still have to maintain contact with them. Most people just can't do it because they run into those mental relationship limits. Creating and building relationships, even weak ones, takes the repeated exposure of consistent contact. And as you move beyond the 150-person limit, it gets harder to add new relationships.

> *Creating and building relationships, even weak ones, takes the repeated exposure of consistent contact. And as you move beyond the 150-person limit, it gets harder to add new relationships.*

Since we don't have the ability to handle hundreds, if not thousands of weak connections, we have to be incredibly diligent to maintain the ones we do have. We have to invest a lot of energy. If we don't, they'll fall to the wayside until some serendipitous event brings us back together again, like a school reunion or a chance encounter at the grocery store. That's why most networking gurus in the past suggested intense regimens of calls, meetings, email, written notes, and newsletters for success. You had to make sure to stay in contact with a large group of weak connections.

My first introduction to professional networking shows how time-consuming this can be. When I started a band in college with my friend Jim, we made a deal. He would work on the songs (which was good because I was a drummer and couldn't read music), and I would book gigs for us. I thought it would be really cool hobnobbing with club owners and other bands; and it was fun, but it was a lot of work too. I would have needed spreadsheet after spreadsheet to keep track of everyone I met, whether they were a booking agent, a band member from another group, or a rabid fan at a show. I should have recorded everything, but I didn't think about it at the time. When I added all these people to the relationships I already had, it took up a lot of my brain space. It wasn't something I could muscle through, even though I thought I could. What was the result? A lot of missed opportunities and fumbling for names when we were at gigs.

Part of the challenge in maintaining a good-sized network comes from running out of time while trying to maintain all of these connections. Let's say you try to double the number of relationships the average human manages. Those extra 150 relationships (if you only talked to them twice a year) would require an extra conversation every workday. That doesn't include all of your other strong connections and the "relating" part of those relationships. You can see where that kind of process would quickly collapse.

Ironically, the people who are the best at reaching out and building relationships aren't usually good at creating structures in their time, so they don't follow a networking regimen anyway. And that's why networking is so frustrating for so many people; it really ends up as a game of chance. You might get lucky here and there, and when things go well, it's fantastic. But it's not consistent. There's this understanding that we have to stay in touch with our weak connections, but that takes effort and time, which is already a precious commodity. It's not from a lack of desire that networking gets dropped to the bottom of our to-do list; it's just that the to-do list is so long already. For most of us, networking falls outside of our job description. We know it's a good thing to do, but it's not what delivers the immediate paycheck.

We lack the right combination of access to new contacts, the structure and attention to devote to cultivating our weak connections, and the time to make it all happen. ARGH! It frustrates me to just think about it.

But at the beginning of the chapter I mentioned that understanding Granovetter's research also offered a way to make networking effective. By shining a light on the power of weak connections, he actually did two things. First, he showed us the value of having a lot of connections, which is a problem because most of us don't have the resources and capacity to create them. The other thing he pointed out is that weak connections have value and that people don't have to be close to help us. We don't need super-strong relationships to find them helpful. Instead of worrying about being everyone's best friend to get value from our network, we just have to find a way to cultivate these weak relationships in an effective and efficient way.

> *Instead of worrying about being everyone's best friend to get value from our network, we just have to find a way to cultivate these weak relationships in an effective and efficient way.*

Professionals who provide services that people need only occasionally—for example, real estate agents, attorneys, or insurance agents—have always built networks filled with weak connections. Since people don't buy houses or life insurance very often, it's more helpful to have a network that is wide, even if it isn't that deep. That's why these fields are traditionally filled with good networkers. If you think of the stereotypical networker who knows everyone, I'll bet dollars to donuts they're in one of these industries. We can take a page from their networking book and look to expand our network. In fact, one of the biggest compliments I get from my friends is when they call me the "Mayor" of Evanston because I seem to know everyone in this Chicago suburb. I'm not everyone's best friend, but I've spent the last ten years expanding my reach by meeting as many people as I can.

We need a lot of connections, but it's okay if they are weak connections. This means that we can change our focus, although it doesn't let us off the hook completely. It doesn't change the fact that our brains aren't wired for this. We need tools that allow us to stay in contact with a relatively large group of people on a regular basis with a relatively small investment of time and energy. We're in luck because for the first time we have easy access to tools to do just that. We have new communication platforms like LinkedIn and Twitter that allow us to keep track of our network in only minutes per day. We have spreadsheets and customer relationship management software to keep track of who we know and what conversations we had. We can reach out to people with email, texts, and status updates in seconds. We have the ability to connect easily with more people, and in doing so it gives us the tools to maintain these weak connections in a whole new way.

We're going to take a quick detour before we look at how technology can give you the structure that you need to make your networking suck less. Up to this point, we've been looking at why you haven't been as effective with your networking as you would like to be. It would be nice to just jump right into the "how to make it better" part of our conversation, but I want to make sure you are ready for it.

There's an *internal gut check* you have to run through first because I have a feeling that there may be a self-identification issue that is holding you back. If you want to become a better networker, you are going to have do things differently. You might have heard the quote (attributed to many different people) that "insanity is doing the same thing over and over and expecting different results." In all my work with professionals, I've found that the ability to change and do things differently is based on how you view yourself in the first place. So before we look at how social media can be your ace in the hole when it comes to networking in the 21st century, you need to take a look in the mirror. Let's talk about how whether calling yourself an introvert or an extrovert is helping or hurting you, and why it's BS anyway.

Chapter 5

Are You an Introverted or Extroverted Networker?

"3 Networking Tips for the Shy"
"How to Succeed at Networking When You're an Introvert"
"Small Talk for the Socially Awkward"

I f you look for networking advice online, these are some of the articles you're likely to find. It's almost become cool to write about the shyest among us; you rarely see corresponding articles to help out the extroverts. Is it because the introverts are holding us back? Have we decided as a collective that the quiet people are what's gumming up the networking machine, and if we can just get them comfortable and competent, then all of us will see a positive bump in our networking?

Possibly, but I think it stems from the fact that many of us perceive ourselves as introverted to some degree. Even those who are very comfortable with others can mentally gravitate to the few times in the past when they were awkward and shy. And it's easy to interpret that shyness to mean that, at some level, we are really an introvert. So it's easy to blame our networking problems on our tendency to *not* be the life of the party.

But is that perception really true? Are most of us introverts or closet extroverts? My guess is that when you sort all of it out, the answer is neither. The distinction between the two, while having some small benefits for our self-identification, is actually not helpful for our networking efforts. It's an artificial delineation, and the only way you are going to get great at networking is to move past it.

Before we get into the nitty-gritty, let me be clear. Even if these distinctions were accurate, I don't know if they'd be relevant. I don't think that you have to be an extrovert to be successful in networking or think that being an introvert makes you better or worse at building relationships. We'll see in a moment that all kinds of personality characteristics can be incredibly helpful in building a network. What I am suggesting is that you have to be willing to get rid of the distinctions completely—at least in your own mind. True success comes from exhibiting behaviors of both extroverts and introverts.

True success comes from exhibiting behaviors of both extroverts and introverts.

We got ourselves into this pickle because the human brain is wired to think in stereotypes and broad sweeping generalizations. It actually helps us in many situations. For example, instead of seeing the nuance and complexity of someone's personality, it's much easier to slap a label onto someone and say that they are shy, flirty, aloof, or the life of the party. We'd like to think that we have the time to delve into the nuance of everyone's personality, but we're usually too busy. It's easier and often necessary to make knee-jerk reactions and then move on. There are so many other things happening in our life that we can't do a deep-dive into the inner workings of everyone we meet.

While they save us a lot of time and energy, these hasty characterizations can have some negative consequences when it comes to building relationships. Because we do tend to judge a book by its cover, we tend to miss out on opportunities because of preconceived notions. But these generalizations also have a much more insidious effect because we make these same quick judgments about ourselves. Just like we don't take the time to understand the nuances of the people in our lives, we often fail to understand the nuances of our own personalities. And so our beliefs about ourselves actually become self-reinforcing patterns. We think the times that we struggle with networking our indicative of our introversion or incompetence. We basically give up on networking because we don't feel we have the personality for it, and because we give up on it, we don't see any results—which confirms our original opinion.

Up to this point, we've examined some of the powerful external forces that have prevented us from being successful at networking, from the make-up of our brains to the organization of our economy. But if you haven't had a lot of success building your network, I doubt that you say to yourself, "Well, I just haven't found the right balance of strong and weak connections in my personal network." Of course not, it's a much shorter path to simply think, "I haven't gotten a lot of benefits from networking, and everybody says it's super-important. It must be that I just don't have the personality necessary for successful networking. I just suck at it."

In a really backwards way, this sort of thinking is actually very freeing—because it frees you from having to do any work. Think about it. People find it better to blame their lack of success on some innate characteristic that can't be changed because then they are off the hook to put in any effort. I encounter it all the time when people learn that I speak and coach on networking. I remember working with a client who complained that she just wasn't good at meeting new people, had never been, and never would be. It took about fifteen minutes for me to realize that she had so strongly identified herself as a shy, awkward introvert that there was no quick fix to her challenge. I could have taught her every elevator speech and follow-up trick in the book, but if she didn't open herself up to change, it wouldn't matter. She actually wanted to argue for her limitations because then she didn't have to do the work.

What she was saying internally and indirectly was, "I'm not wired for networking, and there's nothing I can do to change it. No more awkward networking events or informational interviews that seem to go nowhere; I can just sulk and complain." The idea of being an introvert actually had some nice benefits for the security of the ego. Of course, it also keeps you from developing more relationships and getting the benefits that you could from a robust network of connections, so it becomes a wonderful self-fulfilling prophecy. And this is where most people stop. They wish they could create a strong network, but they feel stuck because they've bought in to the idea that their personality makes them poorly suited for it.

What kind of personality is ideal for being a successful networker? The answer is quite simple: Yours. There isn't a specific personality type that is required for success in networking. Sure, there are some interpersonal skills that make it a lot easier to build relationships that we'll look at in the next section. But let me assure you, they are exactly that—skills. Skills are things you can learn and develop; they aren't about who you are inherently. You don't have to change *who you are* to be more effective at networking. I hope that allows you to breathe a little easier. You can be yourself and be effective.

> *What kind of personality is ideal for being a successful networker? The answer is quite simple: Yours.*

And yet, I know that many people will still have that voice in their head, telling them that they are shy and that there is no way they can be successful. Let me share my opinion again about whether introverts or extroverts are better networkers. Neither—that whole distinction is made up.

How would you even define an introvert or extrovert? Here are a few of the distinctions that I've noticed:

Extrovert	Introvert
Likes to be around people	Prefers to be by themselves
Enjoys meeting new people	Has a close group of friends
Is energized by people	Recharges in solitude
Has more fun in groups	Leans toward 1:1 conversation
The life of the party	A wallflower

So where do you fit in? Are you completely on one side? Or do both sides resonate a bit for you? Are you a little column A and a little column B? If that's the case, then which one are you—should we call ourselves x% introverted? Do you find the answers change depending on the context and what mood you're in? Maybe the answers to this whole introvert/extrovert thing aren't as concrete as we've been led to believe.

One of the biggest challenges in moving past the introvert/extrovert distinction stems from its beginnings. Over the course of the 20th century, we saw the rise of personality tests in business that claimed to be based on science. There was the hope that personality tests could tell us who should be doing what jobs, and how different individuals should be managed. They weren't inherently a bad idea, but people started taking the results as absolute truth instead of the simple guidelines that they were. It was especially damaging because, even though these tests weren't usually based on psychology or science, they sure made it seem like they were.

This doesn't make personality tests a horrible idea, but it does mean that the results should be taken with a grain of salt. In a professional environment, understanding the broad contours of your personality and the personalities of your co-workers can be very useful. It helps us interact with each other in a way that's effective and respectful.

But it can be dangerous when you simply accept those results as gospel truth. For example, there are personality tests in magazines or online that you can do for fun. However, I don't think you'll take the results as a true determiner of your psychological settings. You don't think, "Wow, I scored 19 out of 25 points on this test; that means I'm an ambitious person, or a flirty person, or that I'm organized. I'm going to approach life from that perspective from now on!" It's just something interesting and intriguing that took up five minutes while you were waiting for the bus. You look up the results after the quiz, are amused, and then you move on.

There are many professional tests out there, and I'm sure that you are like me and have run into people who identify themselves as the results of their personality tests (and sorry Myers-Briggs lovers out there—you tend to be the biggest culprits. "Hi, I'm Judy, and I'm an ENFP!") It's common for organizations to have speakers and trainers run workshops to help everyone determine their personality type because the hope is that everyone will interact more effectively. Because these tests are said to be based on science, and therefore must be accurate, it seems like we should really take them seriously. Of course, we're told about how solid the science is by the people who invented the tests—and want to be paid very well to tell you about the results.

Take the Myers-Briggs test, which I just mentioned. It has gotten a good deal of traction in the corporate world, but if you look at the development of the test, there was little psychological underpinning to it. (But there was very good marketing.) Then notice one of their four major categorizations: Introvert/Extrovert. It makes sense that everyone who took these tests started to identify themselves as either an introvert or an extrovert. Even if they just heard about distinction, they identify as one of the two.

We seem to like putting ourselves in easily defined categories, which often becomes a self-fulfilling prophecy. "Oh, of course Bill is a great networker, he is an extrovert, but me, I'm an introvert. I'm shy, so I can't be successful at meeting new people." Keep in mind that when people take different personality tests, or even the same test at different times, they often get different results. This may have happened to you. Is it because the person taking the test is changing or because the test is measuring something that isn't an absolute? There are many more variables than a simple two-choice answer might imply.

Instead of being concrete, these categories are really descriptions of wide spectrums of different behaviors and emotions. Sure, you might know someone who is always 100% internally focused, just like you might know someone who is always talking to other people and the life of the party. Those examples pop into our minds easily because they are rare, and so they stand out. Most of us fall somewhere in between the two extremes. Even for someone who prefers solitude a lot of the time, they probably don't want to be a reclusive hermit and live in a cave.

The results also depend on the context a lot more than people want to believe. It's completely possible for someone to be quiet in one environment and outgoing in another. For example, you might not feel comfortable going to parties but love to entertain your friends in your house. I've often met people who are shy until they're involved in conversation about something they're passionate about—then you can't get them to shut up. Are they an introvert or an extrovert? If someone is nervous in face-to-face conversations, but a prolific contributor to online discussions, are they an introvert or an extrovert? The distinctions fall apart when we try to think of them as rigid categories.

If you want to see this in action, go to a huge fan convention like ComicCon in San Diego. The common stereotype of the nerdy guy who likes comic books is about someone who is shy and socially awkward. Well, at ComicCon, that quiet guy who works in IT dresses up like a superhero and parties with thousands of his closest friends in San Diego. Sure, I'm painting with a broad brush to make a point, but that point is that you can't just ascribe a blanket label to someone's personality based on their behavior in one environment.

> *Well, at ComicCon, that quiet guy who works in IT dresses up like a superhero and parties with thousands of his closest friends in San Diego.*

Use your own experience as a guide. Even if you feel that you fit into one of the categories like introvert or extrovert, are there times when you adopt the opposite persona? Are you usually extroverted but have days where you really don't have the energy to deal with a big group of people? To go back to the example of ComicCon, maybe you are usually quiet and reserved but sometimes find yourself in a setting where you feel comfortable—maybe when you are around your close friends—and are suddenly talkative and highly engaged. When your favorite topic comes up, can you wax poetic for hours?

I've always found the results of these tests for myself very perplexing because I never received consistent results, but that's because I straddle the definitions of extrovert and introvert. People often view me as a natural extrovert because I do well in, and usually feel comfortable with, large group scenarios. But I had a friend point out that just because someone has some social skills, it doesn't mean that they are an extrovert. And when we go back to the lists shown earlier in the chapter, I would say that I am comfortable meeting new people, but I can be drained by large groups and replenished by being alone or with just a few people. In fact, I'm actually okay some days working from home the entire day and not seeing anyone. But I also love public speaking and being in front of large audiences.

I know from first-hand experience that the definitions are a little wonky, and that's why we want to make sure that we don't get trapped by them. I'm sure that you hold a story in your mind about yourself and how you are as a networker. I'm not saying you have to completely re-conceptualize who you are to be successful at networking. Who you are right now is the perfect starting point for being a top-notch networker. But I am saying that the key to building even more success is clearing out conceptions of yourself that might get in the way. Then you can evolve your approach to your networking activities when it's warranted.

When you let go of these labels, you'll also see how being introverted or extroverted wouldn't inherently lead to more or less success with networking anyway. For example, the gregariousness that is associated with extroverts is only a small piece of the puzzle. There's a lot more to this than just meeting a lot of people. Play to the strengths you have instead of jamming yourself into a mold that doesn't fit. If you are better at organization, then focus on a system of regular activities that support building ongoing relationships. One of your networking partners might be better at associative thinking and will be able to make connections between her contacts more easily. There's no right road to success.

> *The gregariousness that is associated with extroverts is only a small piece of the puzzle. There's a lot more to this than just meeting a lot of people. Play to the strengths you have instead of jamming yourself into a mold that doesn't fit.*

Don't get caught up in thinking that you can't be successful at networking because you're just not cut out for it. That is an easy way out; however, most of the reasons you struggle have nothing to do with your personality. They have more to do with those bigger structural challenges we looked at. As we look at ways to move past these and unsuck your network, know that you can't hang on to the old belief that your personality was the reason for your failure. It wasn't your fault. Know that you can take the next step forward, no matter your personality.

Chapter 6

The Social Media

Let's jump back on the path from Chapter Four. We were talking about the conundrum that history and biology had left us. Big networks are more useful, but we can't manage many relationships. Why is this so obvious to us now? The answer is technology, or more specifically, social media. Even though connecting with your network was complex in the pre-internet days, technology has made it much easier to connect and interact with a large number of people. It's our way out of the trap!

So many people want to talk about social media that you can find gobs of information out there about the hows, whys, and whats of interacting online. It's almost as if social media's main purpose is to give people a way to talk about social media. Hundreds of articles are written every day on the blogosphere that give strategies and tactics on how to use these sites; I've even thrown in a few myself. And since the amount of money involved in the social media industry—and it is a true industry—has skyrocketed, there's a lot being said about the companies who deliver it. Facebook, LinkedIn, Twitter, Instagram, and Pinterest dominate the front pages of newspapers, both in print and online. And there are thousands of entrepreneurs trying to invent the next big site. The odds of success are long, but the payoff is so great that it's worth the try.

But what does this really mean for you if you aren't a social media consultant? The world of social media is a whirlwind of activity and evolution. It can be hard to keep up with it, even for those who work in the social media world. For most other professionals who are just trying to figure out how to integrate these new tools into their daily work, it seems well-nigh impossible. From the outside looking in, it looks like a bunch of chaos, and really, who has time for that? When things change at an ever-increasing pace, why bother?

The social media eco-system is evolving so quickly that anything I write is likely to be outdated by the time this book goes to print. Specific instructions on how to use each platform for networking success are better suited for quick-turnaround outlets like blogs and podcasts. We'll look at a few of the main players in the social media world and how to leverage them in the next sections. But before we get there, you'll want to know why social media has shaken things up in the networking game and why it's worth your time.

Let's be straightforward, I'm talking to everyone who's reading this, not just the 50-year-old who thinks that social media isn't for them. There's actually a yin-yang relationship involved in communication on social media. You need to balance understanding the technology with the ability to communicate in a professional setting. One of the biggest misconceptions I hear is that social media is just for the youngsters and that if you aren't a Millennial, it's not even worth trying to figure it out. Sure, if you are under the age of 25, you grew up with social media and are much more comfortable with it. But you also don't have a wide range of experience in communicating professionally. If you've been in the workforce for 20 or 30 years, then the technology might be new and intimidating, but you're much more likely to understand how to communicate with people in a work setting. I've found over and over again that when you talk about using social media for business, age isn't a plus or a minus. What we are talking about isn't technology, it's communication.

And that's the most important theme to keep in mind. At its roots, social media is simply a communication tool. In fact, a simple definition of social media is any Internet platform where the users create content to communicate with each other. Think about it. Facebook doesn't create any content; it gives a virtual wall for people to post information and share with their friends. And that's why we have to wrap our heads around social media—because if networking is all about relationships, and relationships are all about communication, then we have to look at ways to harness the power of these emerging tools.

Social media holds the key to helping us move out of the Dunbar/Granovetter double bind—weak connections in our network hold a lot of opportunity, but we can only manage a small number of them. We need to find a way to manage more connections, and here's where social media's value shines. It gives us a chance to do just that.

> *Social media holds the key to helping us move out of the Dunbar/Granovetter double bind that weak connections in our network hold a lot of opportunity, but we can only manage a small number of them.*

By the way, it's not a specific site that is going to help us, but rather the evolution of our communication capabilities. When looking at how to distill value from our networking, we saw that it had a lot to do with the structure of our network. It was about building up a large web of weak connections that would connect us to other spheres of information. But of course that's hard to do because maintaining this large number of weak connections takes an enormous amount of time and energy, so we just give up.

I've spent the last few years teaching professionals how to use social media, and I have concentrated on how to use LinkedIn. In fact, I heard that LinkedIn calls people like me evangelists because we spread the word about LinkedIn for them. The analogy works because I often had to try to convert people to using social media, especially before LinkedIn became a household name. The resistance had nothing to do with not understanding the functionality of social media. People were just tired and didn't want to have to squeeze even more into their already-packed day. They didn't even want to think about social media because it was just another thing to add to their to-do list.

Unfortunately, that prevented people from seeing the value of social media to do the exact opposite—it actually saves time. What would happen if we had a way to keep in touch with a large group of people with a low expenditure of time and energy? That would solve the challenges of maintaining a large network, wouldn't it? Or at least make it a lot easier. It used to be that we could only share information on a one-on-one basis. One-on-one communication required us to invest attention with a specific person during a specific period of time. When that was over, we could move on to the next interaction. It didn't matter if that was a face-to-face conversation, phone call, or a letter—a 20-minute conversation took 20 minutes.

Before social media, sharing beyond a one-on-one scope required a lot of resources, which is why very few individuals could share information broadly. We used to live in a broadcast world, because most information was broadcast from a few sources to the world at large. Most of the large-scale communication came from organizations that had access to the necessary tools to share widely: newspaper, television, books, radio, mass mailings, newsletters, etc. It was definitely a one-way street and not much of a conversation. Except for the letters to the editor in the newspaper, there wasn't a lot of back and forth happening. And when there was, it was usually a lopsided dialog that had a lot of lag time.

You couldn't really use these communication tools to build relationships. If you were watching a television show, you might want to believe that you had a relationship with the person on the screen, but there wasn't really any interaction. At best, an individual could share their message to the masses, but they couldn't get any feedback from their audience.

We have seen a lot of changes in the 21st century. In television shows like American Idol, the home audience can actually determine the outcome. Even now you can see the lines blurring between movies, books, and videogames. I foresee a future where we tell our grandkids, "When I was your age, we used to watch a movie from beginning to end without having any input," and they'll look at us like we're crazy. In their world, they will participate in the media they consume.

Until now, there weren't many opportunities for the Average Joe to build relationships on a large scale. It took a lot of work and resources that were simply out of reach. If you wanted to stay in touch with people, it was a matter of getting out to as many meetings and social gatherings as possible. At best, you might send a Christmas card to everyone on your Rolodex list, or a holiday card if you wanted to be a little more inclusive. I remember seeing my grandmother—who not only raised seven kids but was also a CPA who ran her own practice—send out those little desk calendars with her name on it to her clients for the New Year. It seems a little cheesy now, but it was her best effort to keep her name in front of her network. There was no easy way to stay in touch with a large group in real time.

Technology helped create the broadcast world, and it also ushered in the current world, which is much more interactive. The first crack came with the development of email. Now people had the ability to send the same message out to a large group of people easily ... and

> *Technology helped create the broadcast world, and it also ushered in the current world, which is much more interactive.*

get a response back in real time. You could add multiple addresses to the same email and send it to many people at once. The structure even mimicked the snail mail idea of carbon copying a physical letter (the now dreaded "cc") that we already used. But instead of using a piece of carbon paper to double or triple the number of copies, we could send the message to hundreds. In a world inundated with social media, this can seem antiquated, but it's easy to forget how powerful this was— and how recent. Email only became popular in the early 1990s. Email also led to the explosion of e-newsletters. Again, they now clog up our email inboxes, so we forget how recent they are and how useful they could be compared to a pre-email world. You no longer needed a lot of resources to share information with a lot of people; all you needed was an email account and a list of addresses.

At the same time, you saw the rise of chat forums in a myriad of different flavors, from some of the original online bulletin boards to Usenet groups that hosted topic specific discussions. I remember sitting in my friend's bedroom in high school and actually dialing in on his modem. Do you remember the screech that made? We would log onto the local bulletin board ExecPC BBS (because the World Wide Web hadn't arrived yet) and talk with other nerdy high school kids like us. The highlight of our week was the Wednesday trivia game, and when I started my first band, I remember hanging out at the Usenet group alt.music.ska. I was reaching out to people around the country and around the world to talk about something that interested me. Just a few years earlier that would have been nearly impossible to do.

When the Web arrived, so did early social media sites like Friendster and MySpace. They took these conversations more mainstream and started embracing people beyond us techno-geeks. And of course, with the advent of Facebook, Twitter, and the business networking giant LinkedIn, social media secured its place on our computers and smartphones— and in our business lives.

We can debate the long-term benefits and challenges of social media use, but for our networking purposes it's a godsend. With each step in the evolution of communications technology, we've been able to have conversations more easily. Even though e-newsletters and online chat rooms lowered the barriers to conversation, it wasn't until we could post short snippets of information in the newsfeeds and on the walls and timelines of our connections that social media became so powerful. It became a tool to converse in the present moment. We moved from the old days when technology supported a unidirectional broadcast to an environment where people could exchange information and engage in conversations in real time.

> *We have moved from the old days when technology supported a unidirectional broadcast to an environment where people could exchange information and engage in conversations in real time.*

One of the biggest complaints about social media is that it doesn't create deep relationships. That's exactly why it's the perfect tool for building a strong network of weak connections; because now it doesn't take a lot of time and energy to maintain a large network of weak connections. You don't need strong connections who know everything about you all the time; it's more important to have reach and a connection that's convenient to maintain. Social media sites, especially those like LinkedIn and Facebook, give you the opportunity to do two important things for your networking.

First, they allow you to share information quickly and easily with a large group of people. We complain about people tweeting from events and not actually participating at the event, but it's actually pretty amazing that you can tell people what you are doing as it is happening. And it also scales these conversations in a way that broadcast technology never could. It takes the same 2 minutes to create a status update on LinkedIn when you have 150 people in your network as it does when you have 1,500. Instead of picking up the phone to have 2-minute conversations with hundreds of people, which would never happen, you can efficiently keep your network in the know.

And in social media, the people you share with have, on some level, opted-in to keeping in touch with you. You aren't just blasting information out in an attempt to get someone's attention. Author Seth Godin talks about the difference between Permission and Interruption Marketing in his book *Permission Marketing: Turning Strangers into Friends and Friends into Customers*. He says that it's much more effective to market to people who have already said they want to hear from you than those you interrupt to get their attention. This is exactly why engaging on social media is so potent. Because we all have significant demands on our attention, trying to share information with strangers takes a lot of time and resources. But because our connections, friends, and followers have agreed to connect with us online, it's much more likely that they'll pay attention to what we have to say.

Secondly, when you flip the process, you now have an easy and efficient way to stay informed about what is happening with your network. Since networking depends on having relationships with people, it's important to remember that it has to be a two-way street. If you're just blasting out information to others, that's not building a relationship or networking, that's just marketing. That's what broadcast media was really good at. What's great about social media platforms is that they naturally aggregate the information we want from the people we want to know about. If you want to stay up to date with your peers in an industry association, you can now connect to them on LinkedIn.

Do you want to know what's happening at a conference? Follow its hashtag on Twitter. Want to see your college roommate's baby's pictures—you have Facebook. Now you can keep your finger on the pulse of your network in minutes a day.

I'm not saying that by posting and reading updates on social media sites that you are having deep and meaningful conversations with your entire network. That would be hard to do because, while technology provides a nice support, we still hit that upper limit described by Dunbar. And would you want to keep up with everything? There really is only so much time in the day. But now you can sustain those weak connections over time with a relatively small energy investment and dive deeper only when you see a reason to do so.

As far as networking is concerned, we need to stop complaining that social media relationships are superficial and transitory. That's why they are powerful. Instead, we should applaud that we now have an expanded spectrum of tools for building relationships. Remember, we still have all the tools—email, phone calls, face-to-face meetings— that we did before. But now we have ways to engage with people in a light fashion and maintain the weak connections that lead to professional networking success. Instead of relying on luck to bring the ideal person back into our life, we can go to our social media networks and do a quick search. And if the ideal person to help is a colleague from a previous workplace, you don't have to call out of the blue. Because it's easier to stay connected on sites like LinkedIn and Twitter, it's much more likely that you have kept in touch. Re-engaging is as simple as dialing the phone and picking up where you left off.

Since we aren't going to evolve new brains in our lifetime, we have to work with what we've got. Looking to outside communication tools is the beginning of the end of our networking woes. Social media and technology act as supports to help us fill in the gaps that biology and history have created. If you have been frustrated with your networking up to today, you're in good company. We've all had the same challenges. But starting today (or whenever you turn to Section II), you are setting out on a new path. Starting today, your network is going to stop sucking and start being awesome.

Section II

UNSUCKING YOUR NETWORKING

Chapter 7

The Path Forward

And that brings us to now. We've examined the long and sordid past of our professional networking efforts. We've seen how the size of our network determines its effectiveness and how our brains are wired to actually prevent us from building big networks. We've looked at how the introvert and extrovert distinctions aren't really a thing. And as far as our networking is concerned, social media is improving the way we interact and can help us move past the limitations of our past. Now that you know the pitfalls and the promises—go get 'em! Attend a bunch of networking events, meet a lot of people, use social media to stay connected, and find professional success as you ride off into the sunset.

If only it was that easy.

Even though it really isn't that easy, taking your networking to the next level can be a lot simpler than you think. We looked at the history of networking to see how we can move beyond the obstacles that held us back in the past. Now that we know what prevented the creation of vibrant networks, we can see what tools we need to fill the gaps. Our mission is to find a way to put all of it together.

Jumping ahead a bit, Section III covers a range of specific tactics and tools you can use when you are networking. Sometimes we just want to know what to focus on, what to say, and what to write. If you are itching to make your next event more effective, then skip ahead and dive in.

But before we get there, I want to look at some strategies you can employ to not only improve your network and your networking, but also to improve *how you improve* your networking. There's a subtle play between good strategy and effective tactics, and when you know how your strategy can inform and influence your tactics, you will be more effective.

People always ask me about the secrets to successful networking. I think they're actually looking for the one or two supposed shortcuts that all successful networkers use. They figure if they know that, then they can skip all of the hard stuff. As if there are any shortcuts! It's like asking a doctor to tell you the one thing you need to do to be healthy. There's a lot more going on than a few sound bites can cover.

But there are some overarching strategies that all successful networkers use in some form or another. Things that can help you get better at networking in the short-term, as well as the long-term. To get the full benefits from your activities and efforts, the way you approach your networking both internally and externally must align. In other words, how you think about networking and what you do about networking have to be in step. Achieving this balance isn't necessarily intuitive, and unfortunately there's no class in school that teaches this. And yet, both your internal and external environments provide the foundation for successful networking.

> *To get the full benefits from your activities and efforts, the way you approach your networking both internally and externally must align.*

You can absolutely skip ahead to look at the tactics in Section III, but in some ways, that's like learning to sing a song in another language phonetically, which rarely leads to nuanced or good music. You'd be going through the motions without understanding why you are doing them, and you wouldn't gain the capacity to improve your networking over time. I want you to be good now, but I want you to be even better down the line.

In this section, you will learn the importance of:

1. Becoming an Autodidact
2. Developing Self-Awareness
3. Working Your People Skills
4. Making Technology Your Friend
5. Approaching Your Business Life Profersonally™

Chapter 8

Become an Autodidact

Confession time: I've always been a fan of so-called SAT words. You know, the big words that no one ever uses in real life that you can only find in the vocabulary section of an SAT test. I know that *autodidact* is not a common word, and when you saw it you may have thought, "What the heck do cars have to do with networking?"

My poor attempts at humor aside, a huge part of being successful in networking involves this principle. To say someone is an autodidact is just a fancy way to say that a person is self-taught. Abraham Lincoln was an autodidact because he had only about 18 months of formal education—but he read widely and continually to supplement his education on his own, enough to become president. You don't find as many autodidacts as there were in the past because our education system is different now, and every child is required to go to school. One of the negative side effects of mandatory childhood education is that most adults never discover how to learn on their own.

This is critical because there really isn't any schooling for the skills you need to become a master networker, and you must learn them on your own. Even though it's a key ingredient for professional success, there isn't a formalized process to learn how to create a robust professional network. The lucky ones among us stumble upon a set of skills that help them out, or they find a mentor who shows them the way. It's rare to find a Networking 101 class that teaches the skills and tools necessary for successful networking—at least I haven't found one yet—so anyone who wants to improve their skills has to learn them on their own.

A big part of this stems from an educational system that is woefully out-of-date. It sets individuals up for failure in today's interconnected world. It's a 20th-century system (more of a 19th-century system, really) that isn't designed to teach the skills needed for our current knowledge-based and relationship-based economy.

If you are like me, your grade-school years were probably spent in a traditional classroom. We sat in rows, listening to a teacher and obediently completing assignments. That's great training if you are going to work as a pencil-pusher in a hierarchical bureaucracy or as a mid-level manager in a factory, but it's not going to prepare you for the chaotic and ever-changing environment we find ourselves in today. We need different skills than professionals did a hundred years ago; we need help with relationship-building, problem-solving, and making creative connections.

To make it worse, when we were in the classroom, we would actually get in trouble for talking to each other. Unless we were working on a group project, there was little interaction with our classmates. (No wonder we're bad at collaboration in the workplace—but that's a whole different book.) Our only opportunity to interact with others and develop our social skills was on the playground or in the cafeteria. But those weren't peaceful environments for learning interpersonal communication skills; they were a hit-or-miss struggle for social survival. I might be overstating that a bit, but really, kids can be pretty tough on each other.

Things changed a bit when we got into higher education, but not by much. For example, in college there was almost no chance to hone and develop new networking skills in the classroom. The classes we took rarely addressed these topics, even though most professionals, regardless of industry, routinely identify these skills as being critical for success. It's ironic that most college students are there because they want to prepare for their future career, but there's no attention given to the soft skills that actually prepare them for that future position. A friend told me about law school and said, "Law school teaches you the law, but it doesn't teach you how to be a lawyer. You have to learn how to interact and negotiate with your peers, your clients, and your opponents. You learn that—hopefully—at your first job."

In the same way, college might teach you the knowledge you need to *do* the mechanics of your first job, but it doesn't teach you what you need to know to be successful once you get there—or even how to get the job in the first place. This is further complicated by the rise of online learning. Students now access classes online around the country and around the world without leaving the comfort of their laptop. On a strictly educational level, that's great, but it doesn't give them much of an opportunity to engage with classmates and practice their relationship skills. And students who opt for a strictly online college experience can get their academics online, but they lose out on the experiences outside of the classroom, like extracurricular activities and dorm life, which are a key part of developing a network in college.

Even if you go to business school, which in theory should teach you about business, there's usually more attention put on building spreadsheets and quarterly reports than on building professional relationships. We've all heard about or experienced the person who is technically competent but horrible to work with. The negativity they bring to the workplace far outweighs their contributions, and they often drive their colleagues away. You'd think that someone with an

MBA wouldn't fall into this category, but it's far from uncommon. It's just as bad, though, when you have a person who is somewhat incompetent but who has good people skills. Everyone likes them, so there's no compelling reason to replace them, but nothing gets done.

So we often enter the workforce without the training and education necessary to successfully engage our colleagues, and we're already working against the evolutionary forces that make us bad at networking. Compound that with the fact that in all our years of education, there wasn't even a cursory attempt to teach us some of the basic skills to help us cope.

But wait! Once we land a job, it makes sense that our employers will help us develop those needed skills. Right?

Nope.

To complicate things even further, our employers are the ones who could benefit the most from our skill development, but they are often the least likely to support that training. And to be fair to them, they are caught in a quandary. They can invest in their employees so that they're more productive, but that also makes them more valuable—to other companies. It's hard for anyone to watch the people they've invested in walk down the block to a competitor. Why spend money that will just walk out the door?

It is also hard for them to invest in developing their employees' soft skills because it's not easy to track the return on investment. There isn't a clearly visible direct correlation between networking and results that can be reported on an annual business plan. When a company prioritizes where to spend their money, it's a lot easier to justify spending it on new computers that have a quantifiable return than on their employees' relationship skills. Ask any manager what they want from their people, and you will hear a litany of crucial communication and soft skills. But it's hard to fight for a training budget when you cannot measure the impact.

It may be easier to deal with employees that have substandard skills. Sure, it leads to diminished capabilities, but it's cheaper and less risky. The status quo may feel a lot safer. We hear about companies that heavily invest in their employees, such as Starbucks and Dell, but the reason we hear about them is because they aren't the norm.

Your employers are faced with a dilemma. They can either train you and help you get better—and increase your flight risk—or they can do nothing and accept what you give them and hope that you'll get yourself to a professional development seminar and get better on your own.

If you're going to get better at networking, you have to do it yourself. You have to be the #1 investor in you. The biggest key to being an autodidact is to embrace the fact that you can become one at any time. You have to embrace the responsibility. You can't expect your training to come from someone else. In this economy, everyone is really working for "You, Incorporated." Even if you get a paycheck from someone else, you'll probably have a number of different employers during your career. And if you are one of the exploding numbers of entrepreneurs, solopreneurs, and small business owners, then you truly are working for You, Inc. If you are working for yourself, and you know that investing in yourself will make you more successful, it's time to start investing.

> *If you're going to get better at networking, you have to do it yourself.*

How do you do that?

There are a lot of theories on how we learn best, but there are a few key elements to keep in mind. The first we just mentioned: You have to take responsibility for your own education. When you accept that the buck stops with you and that your personal development is up to you, it opens your eyes to the possibilities. Once you take responsibility for your own training, you will find opportunities where you can learn.

The second step is to find out how you like to learn. Education for children may be standardized, but when you are an adult, you get to decide what works best for you. You might find live seminars highly stimulating, while your best friend falls asleep halfway through them. I plead guilty to that one; I'm not always the best spectator at conferences. That's why I thought, "If I can't stay focused sitting in the audience, I might as well learn how to be up on the stage." I know some people who can't read a book for more than 3 pages, but if it's an audio book, they will actually sit in their car for an additional 15 minutes after they've arrived at their destination just to finish the chapter. Figure out what you like and press on.

You're reading this book, so my guess is that you like to read, or at least you find it's a good way to learn. If that's the case, you're in luck because there are a host of great books on the shelves these days about how to network. Check out the additional resources at the end of this book for some ideas, or peruse the reviews and comments on sites like Amazon. One of the most overlooked and economical resources for career development is your local library. Look up a few books on networking and relationship building, and then see what books sit next to them on the shelf. Some libraries actually have this as a feature on their websites. Whether you are reading an old-school book, reading on your smartphone, or using your Kindle, there is a plethora of information out there.

And don't overlook the classics. My favorite book about relationships is Dale Carnegie's *How to Win Friends and Influence People*. Even though some of the language is a little dated, the concepts haven't changed. Most books about building a network or strengthening interpersonal skills rest on the foundation that Dale Carnegie built, either implicitly or explicitly. The one you are reading right now certainly does, so you may as well go to the original source.

If you prefer your learning to be more visually stimulating, the Internet is a veritable gold mine. Start by searching YouTube. You will find short tutorials on everything from elevator speeches to using social media to stay in touch with your new contacts. (You might even find a few by yours truly!) There are even full-length seminars and lectures by some of the greats. Another wonderful place to search for broader information on relationships is the online TED talks. Many of the topics, while not directly tied to networking, address new discoveries about how people interact and relate to each other. They can be a wonderful starting point, and you never know how far you can go without leaving the comfort of your chair.

If you prefer to learn by doing, then seize the opportunity to learn to network while actually networking. Find an environment that welcoming to newbies where it's okay to learn and practice your skills while you meet new people. But you have to do more than just show up to improve—you have to make this practice intentional. Structured networking groups like BNI, LeTip, or your local Chamber of Commerce are great places to start. There are hundreds of groups across the country that meet on a regular basis to strictly focus on business networking. These groups often have the veterans take the neophytes under their wing to practice the skills of building a network, such as giving an elevator speech and having one-on-one networking coffees. The way that you choose to learn isn't what's important. The important part is to get to it.

When we talk about the networking skills to develop, what exactly are they? What do you need to be successful? You can start with the tactical tools in Section III, but there's another set of skills that are often overlooked, and they're the foundation of every good networking story. They are definitely skills that only you can teach yourself. Let's take a look at how you can be the type of person that other people want to network with. Let's look at how socially savvy you are.

Chapter 9

Become Socially Savvy

P op quiz: What are people skills?

If you struggle to answer that question, that's okay. "People skills" are kind of like "networking." It's hard to get a concrete definition, but we think we will know it when we see it. We intuitively know when a person has good social skills or when they are a little on the awkward side.

It's a challenge to talk about how to improve our people skills because most people think they already know what they need to know. I've interviewed over 10,000 people in my career, and except for a small percentage of painfully shy individuals, almost everyone thinks they are a 10 out of 10 on the people skills list. I mean, why wouldn't they? We all have years and years of experience dealing with people— we do it every day.

So we have to accept the fact that although we have a lot of experience interacting with others, we still have a few areas to improve. Where should you start to become a more effective networker? The tactics in Section III are effective, but you need the right foundation before you use them. So we start by strengthening that foundation. We need to look at how you interact, how you communicate, how you listen—those things we call your soft skills.

I've always hated the term *soft skills* (as opposed to the hard skills) because our culture doesn't value things that can't be measured. We're inclined to think that anything soft is weak and unimportant. We value hard skills like engineering or computer programming or creating an Excel spreadsheet because those abilities are easy to measure. It's easy to check the *yes* box if the person has that skill or the *no* box if they don't. There's nothing inherently wrong with that, but unfortunately, using the term "soft" can lead to undervaluing our people skills. Can you imagine a successful professional being described as soft? No way.

It's ironic because the most effective professionals are the ones who have highly developed soft skills. Their ability to interact and work with others is usually a key part of their success. Even the most accomplished architect or engineer is only as good as their ability to work with others. Those in charge are often prized more for their ability to lead other people than for their strategic thinking. We actually see the exception proving the rule when we see organizations where the leadership is successful in spite of poor people skills (I'm looking at you, Apple and Microsoft).

> *Those in charge are often prized more for their ability to lead other people than for their strategic thinking.*

The first thing to look at is your social skills. And remember, I'm using the word "skill" deliberately. Skills can be learned, refined, and developed. On the other hand, the word "ability" gives the impression that something is inherent and occurs naturally, whether it does or not. Much of what we do has aspects of both skill and ability. Michael Jordan obviously had some natural abilities on the basketball court, but he honed his skills to take full advantage of them.

Think back to our conversation about the extrovert vs. the introvert. If you decide your success is based on your personality and there's nothing you can do to change your abilities, then you're out of luck if you weren't given the right ones. But things aren't that fixed or permanent and skill-development is the key to moving past any deficiencies we might have. Are some people naturally predisposed to be more or less social? Absolutely. Our personalities are a complex combination of genetics, upbringing, and education. Some people develop confidence at an early age, and it's reinforced over the years. Others aren't as comfortable around people.

You probably know someone who is naturally charismatic. They're the kind of person who gets along with just about everyone and can make friends with a room full of strangers. It's hard to say how much of that is a natural ability and how much is a learned skill, but don't put that person on a pedestal and think, "I could never be that good with people." To look at incredibly charismatic people (think of JFK or Bill Clinton) and use them as the standard is self-defeating. You don't have to be super-charismatic to be successful. Most of us already have the necessary tools to engage with people comfortably and effectively, but first you have to believe that you can move the needle on your social skills. Becoming a master networker doesn't happen overnight, but you can improve your interactions with others.

Because people skills are sometimes hard to define, and the dynamics of human relationships are so complex, it can be hard to know where to focus first. In some ways, you'll spend the rest of your life honing these skills because there's always room for improvement. That being said, here's a list of a few things that can make you more socially savvy:

1. Dress and Grooming

First impressions matter. When we talk about communication skills, most people think of the spoken word—either speaking or listening. But a big chunk of our communication is non-verbal. How you look and act when you're around people is important. We may try to downplay the superficial aspects of ourselves (we say, "It's what's on the inside that counts"), but the way we present ourselves can determine how others respond to us.

When you arrive at a group event or have a one-on-one networking lunch, people will judge you based on your appearance. It may sound harsh, but it's true—and you do it right back to them. It's not even conscious; we are wired to draw conclusions about others through the non-verbal cues of dress and grooming. Not all of these judgments are negative—there's a reason why we dress well when we go to a job interview. We are trying to send a good message by our appearance.

> *We are wired to draw conclusions about others through the non-verbal cues of dress and grooming.*

Our goal is to harness the positive messages we send out on an unconscious level. This doesn't mean you have to become a sartorial wizard (sorry, not quite done with the SAT words). What I mean is that you don't have to look like you strolled off the catwalk at this year's Fashion Week. It's not about being a clothes hound who follows the latest trends from Milan and Paris. You simply need to dress appropriately for the occasion and present yourself as competent and confident. Your manner of dress will be determined by your type of work and your environment. The expectations are different if you're an attorney in Manhattan versus a graphic designer in Austin. Just remember that whether the "uniform" is a gray suit or jeans and a hipster t-shirt, your professional appearance says volumes about you.

I learned this lesson when I first interviewed potential sales reps to join my "blade-slinging team" at Cutco. I was 22 years old and was interviewing people who were frequently my age or older. I needed to establish credibility and authority, and one of the keys to that was how I dressed. Of all of the training talks my first division manager Jeff Bry delivered, the one I remember to this day was "Dress for Success." He taught the basics of how to dress professionally—things like what to look for in a suit and how to match your shoes and your belt. (Remember, I had just graduated from college where my uniform was a daily dose of jeans and t-shirt.) That lesson made a lasting impression on me because I began to understand the powerful message my wardrobe communicated and that I could purposefully manage those messages.

Bringing your wardrobe and grooming habits up a notch or two isn't hard, but you may need to experiment a bit. In the end, you want to be comfortable and have a style that reflects your personality. If you have a friend who always looks good, ask them for tips. You can also get a lot of great ideas online from blogs on style or even social media. For example, Pinterest is a great source of style ideas for men and women. Go through your closest and ask yourself, "If I saw someone else wearing this, what would I think about them?" The next time you're at a professional event such as a conference or association meeting, notice how other people are dressed and the effect it has on you. Think about the impression you want to leave. You don't have to be the best-dressed person in the room. Just make sure your image matches the message that you want to send.

If you want proof of how this works, dress in a suit and go to a large retail store. You will be surprised at how many people ask you to help them because they think you are one of the store managers. A suit is usually worn by someone who is at work and is in charge, and the assumption is that if you are in a store and you are wearing a suit, you're not a shopper, you're an employee—and you probably know where the office supplies are.

2. Body Language

The way we act is another component of unspoken communication. I'm not just talking about the big actions that we do on a conscious level; I'm talking about the host of unconscious behaviors we engage in during interpersonal communication. Studies show that how we carry ourselves has a tremendous impact on others. It can be as be as simple as making eye contact (or the lack of it) or as subtle as the small expressions that flash across our face when we speak. It can be challenging to control all of your unconscious body language—it is unconscious after all—but even small tweaks can have a big effect.

Start with a self-assessment. Think back to the last time you were at a party or group event. How did you carry yourself physically? Did you look people in the eye? Hint: If you want to test yourself, try to remember the other person's eye color. What did you do with your hands when you spoke? Did you wave them all about to prove a point? If so, was that distracting, or did it reinforce your message? If you can't remember, notice how you carry yourself the next time you're in a group.

You don't need to overthink this, but with practice you can use your body to communicate the messages you want to send. For example, if you find that you stand too close to people (if they back away, you're too close), then take a step back. If you tend to hunch over and cross your arms—which can be perceived as being closed off—open your stance to be more inviting. You can also learn how to match the stance and demeanor of the people you are with. This was important for me to learn because I tend to be high-energy and pretty intense when I meet someone new, and I found out that it could make some people uncomfortable. Now I aim to purposefully match their energy level and mirror that back to them. People feel comfortable with people who are like them, which opens them up to be more receptive to you.

> *People feel comfortable with people who are like them, which opens them up to be more receptive to you.*

3. Small Talk

Everyone bashes small talk, and yet, we all do it. I think it gets a bad rap because we usually engage in small talk with people we don't know well and in places we'd rather not be. But if we change the way we think about small talk, we can use it as a powerful tool to help build relationships. Research shows that small talk is actually important to developing relationships. This seemingly inconsequential banter goes a long way to help lubricate the conversation and make everyone feel more comfortable.

You can get better at small talk, even if you're like me and don't follow professional sports or the Weather Channel. Do you have to master a bunch of superficial topics to be good at small talk? Not at all. One of the best ways to improve is to become skilled at asking questions (See more in Section III, Asking the Next Question™). Don't feel that you have to be clever and interesting; instead, turn the tables and let the other person talk. People love to talk about themselves if given the chance—so give them the chance.

I learned this by watching my friend Danny strike up conversations with everyone, everywhere. He was one of my fellow managers at Cutco, and spending time with him was always fun. It didn't matter where we were; if Danny was there, he was going to make friends. I later realized that people gravitated toward him because he was great at making small talk. Most people make the mistake of thinking that small talk is "small" and, therefore, superficial. Danny looked at "small" as meaning short—as in he only had a short time to be in the conversation, and he didn't want to waste any of it.

The key to making small talk is to have a comfortable opener and then ask questions to move into something more interesting than just the weather. Danny started with, "How are you?" like anyone else would, but he would quickly move to, "What do you do when you aren't working that fires you up?" It was a fabulous conversation starter, whether we were at a professional conference or talking to our waiter at a restaurant. Danny learned a lot more about people than he would have if they just talked about a random sports game. He found out what their passion was. And it often took only a minute or two.

Create a list of three to five questions you can ask to get a conversation started, and be sure they are appropriate for the situation. It doesn't make sense to ask someone about their life goals if you just met them at a Chamber of Commerce meeting. Your list could start with:

What do you love to do when you aren't working?
How did you get into your line of work?
What do you like best about the work you do?
What's the most interesting project that you are working on?

Make sure your questions are open-ended and require more than a simple yes or no answer. You're not trying to find out their whole life story, but you are making your small talk about something they enjoy talking about: themselves. Don't forget to monitor your body language. If your posture indicates that you think the conversation is a waste of time (you close your arms, turn away from people, your eyes dart all around the room), they'll think you don't want to talk to them, which is the opposite of what you want. Use small talk to create a climate of comfort so you can dive deeper.

4. Sense of Humor

I'm a little hesitant to put sense of humor on this list, because there's no easy way to define it or give specific methods to improve it. But it's worth mentioning because having a sense of humor is a trait of an effective communicator. I'm not talking about being the class clown or knowing 101 jokes that you can recall at a moment's notice. But there's a different level of connection that develops when people are enjoying themselves. We want to be around people who make us feel good. And even if you don't think you're good at making other people laugh, you can laugh at other people's humor. We love people who make us laugh, and we really love people who laugh with us (not at us).

If you already enjoy a good chuckle a few times a day, you're probably okay. But if you're a little on the stuffy side, you might want to loosen up a little bit. I'm not saying you have to turn into a jokester, but think about the time you spend with your best friends. My guess is that when you go out to dinner, there are lots of humorous stories and smiles that go around. Capture a bit of that energy for your professional relationships. Keep the conversations appropriate, but find the humor and you will find the connection. My good friend, Joe Fingerhut, is a fantastic speaker who works with students across the country. He's also a fabulous entertainer who can juggle, ride a unicycle, and walk on stilts. If you met him, you'd walk away saying he has a fantastic sense of humor. But it's not because he tells you jokes. It's because he laughs at everyone else's jokes, and the laughter is infectious.

Find the humor and you will find the connection.

If you don't know where to direct your humor, point it at yourself. When you're the punchline of your own jokes, you can't offend anyone. But don't wallow in self-deprecating humor—that makes you appear under-confident. True confidence comes through when you don't take yourself too seriously. People like being around others who are positive and sharing good energy. Remember the line from *Annie*, "You're never fully dressed without a smile."

And if you don't think a sense of humor is important, think about this: When women are surveyed about the qualities they want in a potential partner, sense of humor is always near the top—and is often #1. Humor is an important bridge in a romantic relationship, and even though you aren't necessarily looking to find a life partner from networking, you do want to create engaging relationships. I once heard that good communication often looks like low-level, innocent flirting—and that's a pretty good comparison. If you think about it, flirting is simply telling someone that you are interested in them. You can do that in your networking too—just keep it professional and appropriate.

5. Listen

You didn't think I'd have a list of communication skills that doesn't include listening, did you? Listening is by far one of the most critical skills you can develop to become an effective networker. It's ironic that listening is such a common topic when communication is discussed, yet most of us are still pretty horrible at it. Perhaps we don't listen to the advice that says we should be better listeners.

Learning to listen isn't just a feel-good exercise. Remember, we're talking about business, and being successful in business is dependent on gathering information. The knowledge you gather might help you develop a stronger relationship with someone in your circle. Or it could provide information that helps you connect two different people in your network. It could also help you uncover an opportunity. If you don't listen, you will miss it all.

My first sales mentor, Adam, taught me how to listen. It was my first summer as a college kid selling Cutco knives, and I had gotten off to a pretty solid start. Adam tagged along with me on one of my sales calls to give me some pointers. Of course, I intended to show off for him—and I proceeded to perform like a rockstar during the presentation. It was all great, except for the small problem at the end. I failed to make a sale.

I was convinced that the problem was the prospect and that it wasn't a good opportunity, when Adam said, "You did okay, but if it had been me, I would have sold her something." He proceeded to recite everything the prospect indicated through her words and actions that showed she was interested. I had missed every single point because I was too busy concentrating on what I wanted to say instead of what she was telling me.

This was my light bulb moment, when I learned to set my ego aside for the first time and realized that if I wanted to be a good communicator, I had to stop caring about what *I* wanted to say. I had to listen to the messages the other person sent. This realization not only helped me make sales, but it was applicable in my networking relation-

> *I realized that if I wanted to be a good communicator, I had to stop caring about what I wanted to say. I had to listen to the messages the other person sent.*

ships, too, because I learned to listen to my partners and find out what they needed from me.

Don't forget that it's a good idea to listen with more than your ears. The lessons about body language go both ways, and we can learn to "listen" to things like facial expressions, tone of voice, and how someone holds their body to get the big picture. They'll often say things non-verbally that they aren't comfortable saying with their words. Are you picking up on the subtext of your conversations?

There's one more skill that is critical for success. In fact, it's the lynchpin of all of the other skills on this list, as well as any other soft skill you want to develop. But it's not something you'll find in most business books.

You must work to improve who you are as a person.

Chapter 9.5

Personal Development

know that there are rarely half-chapters in books, but this con-
cept is important enough to stand on its own even though I don't
think it requires a full chapter. Personal development encompasses
everything that we touched on in the previous chapter about being
socially savvy. It creates the fertile soil to develop all other skills and
competencies. And though there is more than enough to talk about in
regard to personal development, I'd like to make my point and then
send you on to the many other available resources.

Personal development might seem like an odd topic for a networking book, but it's actually the missing ingredient for most professionals. You can work all you want on your elevator speech, your networking plan, or your LinkedIn profile, but if you have a weak foundation,
none of that matters. That critical foundation is who you are intrinsi-
cally as a person. It's critical to remember that:

Personal development has to precede professional development.
You can only be as good a professional as you are a person.

This actually makes a lot of sense. Effective networking is based on relationships, and relationships are between people—you and someone else. You can't control who another person is or how they act, but you sure can take responsibility for yourself. I'm not saying that you have to be the most amazing person and have it all together before you can be a successful networker. But at some basic level, you want to give yourself a "check up from the neck up" because who you are affects your relationships, both personal and professional. If you're a jerk, or are untrustworthy, or inauthentic, others will pick up on that and your networking will suffer. On the flip side, if you're a warm, generous, and loyal person then you'll probably have a great network even if you don't have the best elevator pitch.

I've met many people who've read all the latest books and have gone to all the seminars on networking, but they aren't good at leveraging these efforts because they aren't good at relationships. You know, those people who talk about themselves all the time, or the ones who are so under-confident that they can't look anyone in the eye. Or the insensitive person, or the oblivious person, or the one who is just too darn loud and demanding of others' attention. These aren't strictly professional problems, are they? You meet these same types of people in your personal life, too, which means that these offensive qualities are part of *who* people are, not a function of their job title or industry.

Hopefully you're not one of them, but here is the truth: All of us have some negative aspects to our personality. Yep, all of us. We may have different backgrounds, upbringings, and education, but we all have things that don't help us with our networking. For most of us, these are only small parts of our personalities, so there's no need to freak out. But these deficiencies do have an impact on how we engage with others. No matter what negative traits we have, they can be improved. And that's the goal—to continually improve the foundation that our networking rests upon.

Here's a sports analogy that shows why this is so important. Let's say you're a professional soccer player. You spend hours and hours practicing dribbling, passing, and taking shots on goal. You sit in team meetings where the coaches break down the next opponent and walk you through specially designed plays so that you can beat them strategically. You know everything you need to know to be successful. But what if you were out-of-shape and couldn't run for more than a few seconds before cramping up? All your skills and planning wouldn't matter if you didn't have the physical capacity to execute them. The strategies we're discussing and the tactics you'll see in the next section depend on your basic fitness, on the personal development work that you've done.

Every analogy eventually falls apart, and this sports analogy falls apart in a good way because sports competitions are just that—competitions. They are zero-sum games that have only one winner. But that's not how life works. In business, there are many winners. Networking is, by its very nature, co-operative rather than competitive. When someone else is successful, that doesn't mean that others lose. When each of us improves, the whole network improves. As the saying goes, "A rising tide raises all ships." Your quest for growth will benefit you and everyone you know.

I'm not going to tell you what kind of person you have to be or that you should be because I don't think it's that cut and dried. Just keep it simple. If you want to be successful at building your network, be the kind of person you'd want to meet. You will be better served if you are responsible, generous, compassionate, respectful, and focused, rather than the opposite. You won't learn these things at a seminar or

> *If you want to be successful at building your network, be the kind of person you'd want to meet.*

conference, and they're not the kinds of things you can pick up from a book, but I can guarantee you one thing: If you become a better person, your networking will improve.

Chapter 10

Make Technology Your Friend

At the same time you're improving your soft skills, we can also focus on some of the important hard skills that are part of any networker's toolbox. We can't forget that even though networking is based on relationships, we also need some technical skills to make life a lot easier. Social media and technology have shaken the networking world in the 21st century, and we can benefit from that disruption if we know what we're doing. There are a number of ways that technology can help us in our daily business interactions, and we'd be foolish to dismiss them.

Technology can be a powerful assistant, but it only works if you know how to use it. Whether we're talking about a telephone or fax machine or email or the latest social networking site, technology can only help us to the extent that we know how to leverage it effectively to accomplish a goal. For example, I could give you the best set of paintbrushes in the world, but if you don't know the first thing about painting, you aren't going to sit down and create a Picasso. In the same way, LinkedIn, Twitter, or the latest app *du jour* won't help if you just stumble around.

So let's look at the ways technology—or more importantly, your technological competence—can help you develop your current relationships, as well as build new ones. The trick is to figure out how technology can serve you, instead of the other way around. You probably already use some form of technology as part of your networking, but do you have a plan for how to use it? Is your technology helping you, or did you get caught in the rising tide and now find yourself chasing the latest gadget or software program? Or does it intimidate you to the point that you avoid it altogether? These seem to be the two main attitudes toward using technology. They each have their good points, and they each have downfalls. Our goal is to find a middle ground that works for you.

> *The trick is to figure out how technology can serve you, instead of the other way around.*

On one side of the fence you have the holdouts who resist any new technology until they absolutely have to use it. These people are reluctant to integrate online communication with their professional life. They shy away from social media now, and even before LinkedIn and Twitter there were some who didn't want to use email or websites. And if we go back far enough, I'm sure you could find certain professionals who hated those new-fangled telephones. The truth is that most of us are smart enough to understand technology, but some of us have an internal block that gets in the way. We make excuses and say we have too much going on, or that we don't want to sacrifice our privacy, or that every new piece of technology is just a fad.

Don't think this is a generational issue. It's easy to suggest that you can't teach an old dog new tricks, but that doesn't stack up against the statistics. The largest growing segment on some social media sites are those who are 50 and up. Everyone uses smart phones, not just

Millennials—and those Millennials can be just as hesitant to use technology as anyone else. I once gave a seminar about LinkedIn for the student athletes at my alma mater, Northwestern University. These were super-sharp, highly disciplined students who had grown up in a world with social media. In the parlance, they were digital natives—people who had never known a world without technology. But they had no idea how to use social media for business because they didn't have any business experience. So let's not assume that we can tell if someone is professionally tech savvy or not by looking at the year on their driver's license. If someone is resistant to new technology, it usually stems from an emotional resistance to change, which usually stems from fear—often of the unknown. And no generation is immune to that.

> *Let's not assume that we can tell if someone is professionally tech savvy or not by looking at the year on their driver's license.*

On the flip side, these holdouts may have an advantage. It might seem odd to praise those who are dragged into using technology kicking and screaming, but I think we can learn something from these people: They don't use just technology for technology's sake. Many people do the opposite and dive deep into that rabbit hole without any forethought; and they spend most of their time playing with a toy, rather than using a tool. We want to keep an open mind about how technology can help us accomplish our goals, but at the same time we also need to focus on the goals themselves, rather than the technology. A little caution may not be such a bad idea.

On the other side of the spectrum are the early adopters and the techie geeks who salivate over every new piece of technology and every new website. To them, technology is a magic pill that will fix everything that is going wrong in their professional life (even if they don't want to admit it). At the extreme, they spend more time mastering the technology than working on their business. It can become a vicious circle—they spend so much time on the tools that they forget what they were trying to accomplish. They don't reach their goals—so they look for the next gadget or website to solve all of their problems. They promptly purchase the new solution and then waste all their time learning how to use it, doing nothing to advance their business. Still no further along, they look for another new tech solution—ad nauseam.

I painted a pretty extreme picture to make a point, but this is a relatively prevalent mindset that stems from the fact that technology has made some pretty big leaps in the last few decades and led to materially significant changes. We are more connected. It is easier to find information. We can automate systems and processes to a degree that was unthinkable 20 years ago. It's not completely absurd to think that the right iPhone app could be the solution to whatever new challenges we face. At best, we become complacent because we're expecting the new thing to do the work for us. At worst, it robs us of hours and hours that we can never get back. And that doesn't even factor in the hard costs of acquiring the technology in the first place.

I've seen this unproductive cycle when working with professionals on their LinkedIn use. Social media has been a game-changer for many of us, particularly for those in sales and recruiting or those who are entrepreneurs and business owners. But most people have little understanding of how LinkedIn works—or how to work it. Instead of developing their skills, they treat it like the baseball field in *Field of Dreams*. They think that if they just show up, all their problems will be solved. The truth is that you have to put in time and effort, and you have to plan first in order to leverage it well.

We have to be cautious, but don't become a Luddite! (Luddites were anti-technology agitators in 19th-century England. It's fun to give your friends a hard time by calling them Luddites). This middle ground can be the difference between being a little bit successful and a lot successful. The trick is to find the balance. That perspective—that technology can be an important tool when it's used in the proper context and with the proper training—is one we want to cultivate. Being technologically savvy means that you recognize a problem, and then figure out how technology can help you solve it. Need to find new prospects? Maybe social media is the answer. Looking to build your professional reputation? Then maybe it's time for a well-written blog or a monthly e-newsletter. It's all about leverage.

> *That perspective—that technology can be an important tool when it's used in the proper context and with the proper training—is one we want to cultivate.*

When we look at how various technologies can help, keep in mind that there isn't a right way to use technology for networking. What's right for you may be different from what's right for somebody else. It depends on your own comfort level with the tools and what your goals are for networking. Used properly, technology can fill the functional gaps in your networking. So if a technology product doesn't solve a problem, then don't use it. It's foolish to invest time and effort on something you don't need.

You don't have to buy all of the latest gadgets, have the newest apps, or spend time on all the trendy social media sites to be successful. But there are a number of networking tasks where technology is the perfect assistant. Here are some tools you'll want to incorporate:

1. Social Media
2. Written Communication
3. CRM/Databases
4. Email/E-Newsletters
5. Video

1. Social Media

Mastering social media is a great goal, but with its continual and rapid evolution, I'm not sure you can actually master it. Unless your job title has "Social Media" in it, it's better to learn targeted methods to leverage social media than to master all of its nuances. In Section III, you'll find some "how to" tactics for a few of the better-known sites like LinkedIn and Twitter, but I won't attempt to extensively cover the sites you should use and how you should use them because any information put in print would be out of date before I could publish this book.

The social media world moves fast. Platforms constantly evolve, new players consistently enter the field, and existing sites wax and wane. (Remember Myspace?) The big gorillas in the room—Facebook and LinkedIn, for example—are hardly untouchable. They are barely a decade old, and there's no precedent for what will happen as they (and how we use them) evolve. It's much more valuable to understand the best practices for using social media. That way, no matter what the predominant social media platforms are, you'll have the confidence to adapt. So instead of trying to understand how to use every site, here are a few overarching guidelines to follow in your approach to social media.

Learn the basic functionalities of social media sites. No matter what site you are looking at, there are many common aspects to them all. Wrap your head around the foundational pieces that you find on most sites, like how to create a profile, how to connect with other users, and how to post content. You don't have to learn every trick or know what every button does. When you know the basic structure of these sites, you can adapt to other social media platforms as they emerge.

Keep your networking goals in mind. One of the biggest complaints about social media is that it's a time suck. It absolutely can be if you are not clear about what you are trying to accomplish. Be very clear about why you are using each site so you don't jump down the rabbit hole and find yourself in front of the computer for hours without accomplishing anything.

Add one platform at a time into your mix. If you're excited about the possibilities of online social networking, it's tempting to join five or ten sites right away to dive in. Keep in mind that it takes time to use these sites effectively and it's counterproductive to create a presence that quickly becomes stale. It's better to spend your time in a few places and really engage there, instead of using many different sites.

People often ask me what sites I use and how much time I spend on social media. The answer is, "A lot less than you probably think." I'm a huge fan of social media; I speak about it regularly and train others how to use it for business. But like most of us, I do have other responsibilities that I need to pay attention to. I leverage social media to accomplish what I want in the least amount of time. LinkedIn is an important platform for me, and I use it daily, but only for about ten minutes. I spent time in the beginning to develop a robust profile, and now I use it to check in on my network. I also write blog articles and create YouTube videos, and I use LinkedIn and Twitter to share that content with my network. And, like one out of every seven people on the planet, I do have a Facebook account. But for me, it's not where I communicate with my business network. When I need a few minutes of down time, I go to Facebook to see if there are any good photos of my nieces and nephews or funny kitten videos.

But that's it. Most of my networking happens in the offline world. Of course, that's not how everybody does it, and that's okay. I have a client who is a corporate recruiter, and he spends about 30–40% of his day on sites like LinkedIn, Twitter, and other industry-specific networking sites, which makes sense because he's looking for candidates so he can fill open positions. Is his way right or is my way right? Neither. They both work for us. I also know a professional photographer who spends a lot of time on Instagram. That makes sense for him because he works in a visual medium, but it would be a waste of time for me. Keep in mind, if you tie your goals to how you use social media, you'll be on the right road.

2. Written Communication

I'm not a member of the grammar police, but I am holding back the urge to admonish you to use "to," "two," and "too" correctly. And avoid flipping "then" and "than." A majority of our communication is still through the written word, and just like people judge us on how we speak, they also judge us on what we write. While we don't necessarily think of writing as technology, it's still a tool we use. The ability to crystallize our thoughts and deliver them on paper, on a billboard, or by electrons is pretty huge.

That power comes with an asterisk. Writing isn't an inherently human skill; you have to learn how to do it well. More importantly, you have to be able to organize and communicate your thoughts effectively. I'm not talking about becoming the next Shakespeare. Your goal should be to feel confident and comfortable sharing information in any written platform. Your effectiveness in using social media earlier is dependent on your ability to write clearly. Whether it's a blog post, a 140-character tweet, a sales email, or a quick text to a networking partner, good writing skills will pay you back over and over.

You might be surprised to learn that my college degree is in history, not in business or something a little more "practical." That turned out to be a really fortuitous decision. Beside the fact that I can talk about some pretty random topics at dinner parties ("Anyone want to discuss the similarities between the growth of the Roman and American republics?"), I had a lot of opportunity to write. And I mean *a lot.* But it wasn't just writing for writing's sake; I had to organize my thoughts and make a clear and coherent argument. Do you think that makes it easier to write a sales letter or an article on LinkedIn? You better believe it. People always ask how a history degree has helped me in my business career. All my smart-aleck responses aside, the best thing I learned was to write well.

How do you get comfortable with the technology of written communication? Do it. Writing isn't natural for most people, so practice helps. There are a lot of great resources online and in bookstores that can help you. In fact, there are a lot of resources specifically geared toward business writing. A few foundational areas you should pay attention to: Develop a solid understanding of grammar. It sounds boring, but do you know what isn't boring? Having someone understand what you say. It's also worth your time to learn about the etiquette for different situations and platforms. Writing an email is different than a LinkedIn status update, which is different than a text. And it won't hurt to brush up on your proofreading. It's amazing how much miscommunication and embarrassment could be avoided if people learned some basic editing skills. A great place to start is to get into the habit of re-reading your emails and social media posts before you hit the send button.

And speaking of writing, a little piece of technology is the business card. While they seem so "old school" that we shouldn't even consider them technology, business cards are a valuable part of any networker's toolbox. We may dislike the image of the networker indiscriminately passing out cards, but that doesn't mean we shouldn't use them ourselves. Not having an easy way to share contact information when you meet someone in the real world can be a problem, so always have yours on you. Too often, people worry about making their cards memorable and creative. It's much more important that your card looks polished and professional and that it is clearly layed out. Include your company and title, your email address, and your phone number. I suggest just one phone number, not four which will make the person have to hunt you down. Keep the cards you receive from others, even if they're in a jumbled stack in your desk drawer. You never know when you might need that contact information.

3. CRM/Databases

You're going to meet a lot of people, and one of the biggest challenges is to remember the details of all these relationships. That's why some of the most common professional software programs on early computers were Customer Relationship Management (CRM) systems. They were databases specifically geared toward tracking people and interactions, and almost every salesperson had one. Since networking is a form of sales, CRM systems can also help us with our networking. They give us a way to outsource our memory. Just like we use Google to remember what actors were in what movies, we can let our computer track our connections and our conversations, instead of trying to keep them in our head. The bigger our network, the harder it is to manage these relationships on our own, and the more a CRM system can benefit us. (Remember that pesky Dunbar's Number.) If you want to have a robust and large network, you'll need some help.

> *Just like we use Google to remember what actors were in what movies, we can let our computer track our connections and our conversations, instead of trying to keep them in our head.*

Your CRM system can be as simple or as sophisticated as you want it to be. You can keep it basic and use a spreadsheet in Excel or even a Microsoft Word document. You can also purchase involved and detailed software programs like ACT or Salesforce. And there is a plethora of middle-of-the-road solutions, many of them web-based, like Highrise or Zoho. We're also seeing social media sites like LinkedIn create CRM functionality within their platform, so you could even use that.

In fact, even though it's not cutting edge or as sexy as a lot of the newer options, I still use Outlook to track all of my networking connections. I enter all of my business cards into my contacts (I've considered getting a business card reader, but I type pretty quickly and it's another impression of their name on my low-tech brain). I use the tasks feature to remind myself to reach out to people to schedule coffee or to keep in touch. The few minutes that it takes for me to enter the name, title, company, email, and phone number are a good investment in relationship-building. I also jot a shorthand note about where I met the person. It works well for me because I also use Outlook for my email and my calendar, and I like having everything in the same place. Let me be clear: I'm not saying it's the perfect system; it's just the perfect system for *me*. Selecting a CRM is kind of like finding a husband or wife. It doesn't matter if it works for everyone else; it just has to work for you.

> *Selecting a CRM is kind of like finding a husband or wife. It doesn't matter if it works for everyone else; it just has to work for you.*

Here are a few things to keep in mind when looking for the perfect match.

Pick a system that you will use. It sounds obvious, but I know more people than I'd like to admit who have the latest and greatest programs and fancy business card scanners but still have a stack of business cards that they haven't entered. They wait for a "free moment" to enter the data, which often never comes. If you have the ability to track all your conversations with your networking partners—and all the ideas that come from those conversations—but you never get around to putting in those notes, then what's the point? You've received zero benefit from that system. I will always suggest a simple and usable system over one that allows you to track every little bit of information but is hard to use. The best systems have as few barriers to use as possible.

There are a few important pieces of information you need to capture. The first is obviously contact info. It helps to grab both old-school information like a mailing address and phone number, as well as new information like social media profiles. If you want to use technology to capture the information, you can use programs like Evernote and CardMunch, which allow you to take photos of business cards and enter the info into your contact database. Awesome!

You also want to track the conversations that you've had and record a few sentences about what you discussed. All good systems have some sort of reminder tool to jog your memory about when you should reach out again. It might not be for months, but it's good to have a tool to remind you when it's time.

Finally, allow enough time to enter all the information, which won't take that long if you schedule it into your calendar. I find it's easiest to make it a set process in your schedule. I personally schedule 15 to 30 minutes the day after attending a networking event (or longer if it's a day-long conference) to enter the new connections I've made. I put in their contact info, send a quick follow-up email to say hello, and reach out on LinkedIn if appropriate. I have a friend who runs a small insurance agency, and he has a different approach. He and his entire staff have scheduled time every Friday morning to enter all of the networking activity from the week. A set process will make it a lot easier to stay disciplined and prevent a backlog.

Whatever your system is, get comfortable with it and use it.

4. Email/E-Newsletters

Email has come a long way since the days of AOL. People thought that the rise of social media might herald the end of email communication, but my inbox begs to differ. Email is a powerful communication tool because everyone has it and everyone uses it. Some professionals only check LinkedIn once a month and rarely check their voicemail, but they still jump every time they hear the ding of an arriving email. You're probably pretty grounded in using email because you use it all the time, but it's worth looking into some of the ways you can use it to specifically support your networking.

The first thing to remember about email is to take care of the little details. Is your name listed clearly? For example, I've seen too many people who have their name pop up as all capitals or all small letters. Sure they stand out—because they look like they don't know how to type. And use your email signature to your benefit. Stay away from pictures of kittens and the abstract quotations from your favorite transcendentalist philosopher. Be sure to include your phone number and links to your website or social media profiles.

It may sound like a small thing, but take another look at your email address. If you work for a large company, you likely have a company-issued address and have little control over it. But if you are running your own business or are independent and have to supply your own email, it can be worth the small expense and learning curve to get an email address with a personalized web domain (yourname@yourdomain.com). It will take you less than an hour to get set up with one of the main domain/hosting providers. If you don't have your own domain, at least get a Gmail address that is yourname@gmail. Every time I meet someone with an aol.com, yahoo.com, or hotmail.com address, it screams "unprofessional" and indicates the opposite of technological savviness. I know it's convenient to use the same account you've always had, but it makes me think that you're stuck in 2002.

One of the best uses of email for networking is the quick follow-up message. When it would be nice to send a quick handwritten note but you don't have the time, send a quick email. After you meet someone new, compose a quick message that says it was nice to meet them. Of the thousands of people I've met through my networking efforts, I've only had a handful send a follow-up email. It's so easy to stand out with just a little bit of effort because most people don't even put forth that little bit. If you see someone's name mentioned online, if they come up in a conversation, or if want to thank them for a referral, drop them a quick email.

> *One of the best uses of email for networking is the quick follow-up message.*

Because one of the biggest obstacles to sending emails is the time it takes to write them, I suggest you have a few email templates you can use for the common messages you send. For example, if you go to an event and meet five new people, you might not think that you have time to write five follow-up emails, and so those business cards sit on your desk where they are joined by seven more after the next event and by yet another card after you meet someone at a friend's party. Pretty soon you have a tall stack of cards on your desk that gets moved to a drawer because they're in the way—and then all those contacts are quickly forgotten.

A lot of the emails I send follow the same format, so I can keep them saved as a template in my outbox. Whenever I need to send a new one, I simply customize what I sent before and send. They go something like this:

"Hi _____.

It was great meeting you at _____. I hope you made some good connections/enjoyed yourself/had fun at the (event).

I've put your information in my "database" and will be on the lookout for you. If you come across anyone who would benefit from working with a business coach or needs a networking speaker, I would appreciate you connecting us.

If there is any way I can be of service in the future, please let me know.

Have a RockStar Day!

D."

I find this simple and effective. If I have more time, I try to customize it with a link to an article on a subject we talked about or an interesting blog post, but that's only if I have time. I would rather get a light touch out to someone than nothing at all. If you make it easy on yourself, the likelihood that you'll follow through increases.

Consider sending a group email or e-newsletter to your network on a regular basis. Most people think they can only send a newsletter out if they run their own business or are trying to sell something. But email newsletters are an easy and cost efficient way to share your expertise with your network, no matter what your job title. Years ago, I signed up for speaker Joe Takash's Quickster list, in which he shares three inspirational quotes every Friday. Simple, fast, and years later he is still on my radar. And it works for him because he speaks on inspirational topics. I know a number of authors who also send out regular emails to their network that are a few short paragraphs on how to write, edit, or be more creative. I have lawyers in my network who send out emails on estate law reforms or how to handle property tax changes. The realtor who helped me buy my condo still sends regular emails—not about what houses she is trying to sell, but about ways I can make my home more valuable. It's an easy way to stay "top of mind" with your network.

Here again, ease is critical. You don't have to send a newsletter out every week or every month—even once a quarter can be useful. Pay attention to content your network finds valuable. It can be content you create yourself, or if you don't have the time, you can share information you've found somewhere else (with attribution, of course). There are a number of e-newsletter services available—like MailChimp, Constant Contact, and StreamSend—that are relatively inexpensive for smaller email lists, which makes them perfect for emailing to your network. They all have simple templates you can use to make your email look pretty and easily digestible—and professional. Don't be upset if everyone doesn't read every part of your e-newsletter; the most important goal is to get your name in front them.

5. Video

Why is video on this list? As of the writing of this book, 72 hours of video are being uploaded to YouTube every minute. That's a lot of video! This is where technology has really changed the landscape of content creation. In the past, the only way to create video was in an expensive studio with expensive equipment and expensive editing. And the only place you could watch it was on broadcast television, or maybe VHS or DVD. Now it's possible to create, edit, and distribute a video with the technology that you literally have in your pocket. And with the increasing presence of the Internet and mobile technology, people want to receive content in video form.

So how about sending a video message to your network? Instead of an email or a written birthday or holiday card, how about sending

> *Now it's possible to create, edit, and distribute a video with the technology that you literally have in your pocket.*

a short, personalized video? It's like a live phone chat that they can listen to whenever they want. Becoming tech savvy with video means a few different things. First, there is the logistical process of recording video. You want to get comfortable with the basics of shooting video. You don't have to become the next Steven Spielberg, but you want to understand the basics of how lighting, sound, and camera technology work. You need to know enough that you don't create that video that we've all come across—the one where you can't see the person because their face is in a shadow or the horrible microphone on the camera doesn't pick up anything they say. Making fun videos on your webcam is great for your personal life, but you want to make sure that any video you create for business has a professional sheen to it. Learning the basics of editing can't hurt because you want to put this all together in an attractive way.

An easy and quick way to do this is to outsource your videos to a professional. In fact, there are probably a number of affordable freelance professionals in your area who will make your video look great. But something you can't outsource is your on-air performance. If you want to get a leg up among other professionals and have an amazing tool to share your content with your network, develop your proficiency in front of a camera. It's not as easy as it looks. The goal is not to be an actor or on-air talent; the goal is to present yourself onscreen as a competent professional. Find opportunities to record yourself in professional situations. Make short videos for your blog or do interviews for online news outlets. Even if you are just recording them for yourself, practice helps a lot.

A few years ago, I started making online videos to post to YouTube. My good friend Rob was an experienced videographer and editor, and he agreed to help me out on the weekends. We turned my living room into a mini-studio with lights we bought at Home Depot and a jury-rigged backdrop. (We hoped my upstairs neighbors weren't home because the creaking floor would interrupt the shoot.) These early videos taught me two things: #1) You can't just wing it. I thought that because I felt comfortable speaking in front of people that I would be fine in front of a camera. Not even close. I spoke too quickly, I mumbled, I said "um" a hundred and seven times in the span of three minutes. It was painful to watch. But—and here's where #2 comes in—I got better when I watched the videos because I knew what to improve. They were a valuable tool for not only my "on-air" speaking, but my public speaking in general.

And that is why I love video. It's great for sharing information with your network, but also great for improving your presentation skills. If you want to see how you look to other people when you speak to them, simply take a quick video of yourself with your phone, tablet, or camcorder. Give your elevator speech or talk about what you do professionally for a few minutes. You can even have a friend or colleague that sits off-camera and interviews you, and then watch what you recorded. Maybe you'll be a natural and it will look fantastic. More than likely, you'll be like me and will find out how you mumble, fidget, don't make eye contact, sway on your feet, are too quiet, or—well, you get the point.

If you are going to be on camera a lot or you have some areas that need improvement, it might be worth getting some outside help on your delivery skills. If you want to get experience speaking in front of people, one of the best paths is to join your local Toastmasters organization. Many of your issues on-camera will be general presentation issues, and the support and speaking opportunities provided through Toastmasters will make you confident and competent.

If you are looking for more specific recording help, you might want to find an acting coach, one who specifically works with actors when they go from the stage to the screen. Working with a camera can be challenging, even for professionals, and you can get great guidance from a coach.

That might feel like a lot of different balls to juggle, and in some ways it is. Remember that the goal isn't to fill up your time with technology, but to use technology to help you accomplish what you already want to do. If you ever feel like the technology thing is getting out of control, take a moment and step back. Take a few days away from social media or put an autoresponder on your email that says you will be returning emails next week. This is a marathon, not a sprint, so take your time. There is no one-size-fits-all solution for using technology to be a successful networker, and there's no deadline you have to meet. When you develop your savvy, you'll figure out how technology can plug into your any of your activities.

> *There is no one-size-fits-all solution for using technology to be a successful networker, and there's no deadline you have to meet.*

Chapter 11

Live a Profersonal™ Life

O ur last topic is a piece of mental technology, and when you first hear about it, you'll think, "Oh, yeah, that makes perfect sense." You'll think it's obvious. But when you dive into what it means to live a *profersonal*[1] life, you'll see that it's actually hard to embody because it's the opposite of how we've thought in the past. You're going to have to buck the habits you've already developed in your networking thought process. The term *"profersonal"* comes from my friend, author and entrepreneur Jason Seiden, who was smart enough to identify (and prescient enough to trademark) it. He called the breakdown of barriers between our personal and professional lives *profersonalism.*

Why is this even an issue in the first place? It's simple. Humans love to compartmentalize. Whether it's genres of music ("excuse me, where's the Norwegian death metal?") or different types of restaurants ("I'd like to have fine-dining Brazilian-Japanese fusion cuisine tonight"), we love to put the pieces of our life into boxes. And that's completely okay because this makes it a lot easier for us to navigate the world. If we had to analyze everything we encounter from scratch, life would be exhausting. We'd be constantly evaluating and describing. It's

---

1   *Profersonal* is a registered trademark of Brand Amper LLC

much simpler to have pre-conceived notions, and that's not necessarily a bad thing. Just finding a movie to watch or job to apply for would take hours, if not days, because we'd have to classify everything from the beginning.

Categorization makes it easier to process the world. Our brains can find information quickly and then move forward. Can you how imagine hard it would be to find a book at the library if there weren't categories or alphabetization? We hear that we shouldn't judge a book by its cover, but in reality we judge everything all the time. It just makes life move a lot faster. And 99% of the time those judgments are correct. As the amount of information we have to digest has increased, we've made even more general assumptions about our environment—and the people in it.

When the number of people we encountered routinely grew beyond that magic number of 150, categorizing them made it easier to navigate through our relationships. It worked for everything else in our lives, so why not put people in different sections in our minds based on what part of our lives they inhabited? We separated the spheres of our lives, and put up dividing lines in our minds. We kept our work relationships separate from personal relationships, and these divisions gave us a shorthand for how to interact with each person. If they were in a work silo, we would engage with them one way, and if they were in the personal silo we would engage in a different way. It allowed us to have shortcuts in how we related to our network. So far, so good.

But, Houston, we have a problem. Though it isn't entirely bad to create categories in our mind, we can easily fall into a trap. We can mistake the artificial mental divisions that we create for something real. We start to think that the people in our lives are actually separate and that we have to keep personal and professional relationships apart. That's not really how it works, but pretty soon we could start focus-ing on the differences instead of the similarities. We start losing out on the ability to make connections, which is really where the power of networking lies. This is a social force that hurt our networking in the second half of the 20th century. We tried to keep the different areas of our life—and the people within them—totally separate.

What's ironic is that the real world never had these hard divisions in the first place. We had clients and work colleagues that became friends over the years. We had office romances, which are the pinnacle of bringing our personal and professional life together. Or we'd help our brother-in-law get a job at our office. We'd volunteer for a non-profit organization or a civic group and end up doing business with the other members. So even though we thought that we left the office at the office and our home at our home, it never really worked that way.

That's why it can be confusing to develop a more decidedly *profersonal* network. On one level you already live your life this way. You naturally have situations where the different areas of your life are combined, but on another level, you think you have to keep these people separate. It makes sense that your brain to get a little jumbled from this. Our goal is to remove the confusion, because in a *profersonal* world there are no clear cut lines between different groups. There are a lot more similarities between how you interact with each separate group than there are differences. You want to bridge those divisions and recognize what they have in common. We have to wrap our minds around the idea that we can purposefully mash up the different pieces of our life. When you embrace this idea, you will see your networking efforts thrive, and it will be a lot more fun.

Let's push the metaphor a little bit more. An emergent music form is called the "mash-up." Instead of creating a piece of music from scratch, mash-up artists take separate pieces of music and put them together in new and often very interesting ways. Think of an artist like Kid Rock, a hip-hop artist turned country singer, who takes two songs from the 1970s: Warren Zevon's "Werewolves of London" and Lynyrd

Skynyrd's "Sweet Home Alabama" and creates a #1 hit song with All Summer Long in 2008. Something new from something old. Many artists will even mash up their own music, and they sometimes bring in artists from different genres to help them recreate and reimagine their music. In this way, they take something old and make something new. At its best, a *profersonal* network is one where you've mashed up all of your different connections into a new entity.

I'm not saying that you can simply snap your fingers and change your mindset, but all you really need to do is change your outlook. Since the divisions we've created between the parts of our lives are mostly artificial, there isn't much you have to change physically to approach your life profersonally. But you can accelerate the process.

You can start with how you label your relationships. The words we use have power. For example, stop calling your friends from your professional sphere your "work-friends." Just recognize them as friends. This will help you break down the segmentation in your mind. Compartmentalization begins as a mental construct, so we have to make the mental shift first. Keep broadening the definitions of your relationships. You can also pay attention to the relationships you already have that span different areas of your life. Do you enjoy spending time outside the office with any of your colleagues? Was your real estate agent your cousin? Did you meet your significant other at a networking mixer? These kinds of relationships already exist, so you can use them as proof that you are already living a *profersonal* life.

In fact, breaking down the barriers between my personal and professional life is how I got my nickname. The name "D. Fish" is definitely not something you come across on a regular basis in the professional world. It was actually a name that my bandmates called me onstage—I used to rap a bit and they jokingly called me MC D. Fish. When my team of assistant managers at Cutco came to our shows, they overheard this. They started calling me D. Fish at the office, and the sales reps picked up on it. Remember, we worked mostly with college students, so it worked well for that atmosphere. Then the other managers and staff overheard this at conferences and started using the name, too. And when the president of a $200 million+ company calls you D. Fish, you know it's a name that is going to stick. It actually worked for me because having this name allowed me to combine two important parts of my life in a way that was natural to me.

Another way to combine the different parts of your life is to find ways to connect the people in your network—especially from disparate social circles. Connecting people is one of the most rewarding parts of networking. Remember the power of weak connections? They are valuable because our weak connections have access to spheres of information that we don't. Weak connections often act as bridges into new areas; and when you connect people, you become that bridge. You create value by connecting two different groups and two different pools of knowledge.

> *Weak connections often act as bridges into new areas; and when you connect people, you become that bridge.*

We already do this in situations when it's an obvious match. We say things like "I was talking to my friend who is an out-of-work graphic designer at lunch, and then I remembered an email from a contact whose company is looking for a graphic designer." That's an easy lay-up, but we can make this an intentional habit. We can be proactive, and look for ways to connect our connections.

When you look at your network, who can you put together? Are there people who have shared interests and hobbies in different areas of your life? At one of my birthday parties, my brother-in-law got into a conversation with a friend of mine from my work in the Young Professionals of Evanston. They were both in the real estate business, but in Milwaukee and Chicago, respectively. That conversation started a relationship where they referred business to each other.

Even if it's not directly work-related (especially when it's not directly work-related) making these connections can be valuable and fun. If your co-worker and college friend are both huge fans of foreign films, they'll probably have some fun conversations where they regale each other with their favorite directors. And who knows where the conversations will lead. Maybe they'll start the next big cinema blog.

All you have to do is shift from seeing the differences in your network to looking for what those people have in common. Instead of viewing them as separate groups, figure out what links them together. You've probably heard that you find whatever you are looking for, so your mission is to find those similarities and make the connections. This is where your listening, creativity, and problem-solving skills can work in sync to bring different groups together.

> *From business partnerships to personal partnerships—and everything in between—it's great to see that new relationships can be created when you bring seemingly unrelated people together.*

I've always been a connector, and I love to introduce people from my different personal and professional circles. My favorite venue for this has been my barbeques. I love to entertain during the way-too-short Chicago summers and regularly invite a mix of friends, clients, colleagues from civic organizations, along with my neighbors. I learned this from Keith Ferrazzi's book, *Never Eat Alone*, and I use my cook-outs to mix my different social circles because it's fun and rewarding to see the new relationships form. I enjoy putting people from the different parts of my life together to see what comes up—and lots of good things have. From business partnerships to personal partnerships—

and everything in between—it's great to see that new relationships can be created when you bring seemingly unrelated people together.

As you embrace the *profersonal* life, keep in mind that it takes a little more effort to manage relationships in a network that doesn't have clear boundaries. As we get rid of those divisions, we have to be a little more conscientious in our relationships. One of the benefits of those hard boundaries was that we knew how to interact with each separate group. Now we have to be a little more conscious of our behavior to be sure it can pass both the social and professional test. We must be much more aware of what we say and do. We have to redefine and restructure some of our relationships, which means we have to be more intentional.

This can be exhausting if you have to keep it top-of-mind on all occasions, which is why I brought up personal development a few chapters back. Now you see why it's so important. You have to be the same person wherever you are, whether it's in the office or at a ball game. And that means you need to be the authentic you when you are in a business meeting, and you probably also need to focus on being the best you when you're at the ballpark. Finding the authentic you that can be present in all environments is an ongoing but valuable process because when you're comfortable with who you are, no matter where you are, you can focus on the people you are with.

> *Finding the authentic you that can be present in all environments is an ongoing but valuable process because when you're comfortable with who you are, no matter where you are, you can focus on the people you are with.*

This personal awareness will also help you manage the inter-personal dynamics of a *profersonal* network. Unfortunately, not everyone is going to be comfortable living in this interconnected environment. Some people like to have boundaries because they aren't capable of jumping or willing to jump from situation to situation without a mental map that tells them how to behave. It's critical for you to respect others' boundaries. Even if you like to break down barriers, your networking partner might not. That's why we often hear the warning to stay away from topics such as religion and politics. It can be hard to broach topics where we have different opinions and still maintain the strength of the relationship. Until you know someone very well, and you know that they can handle a difference of opinion, it's best to stay away from those subjects.

I once spent an evening in Manhattan with a client of mine and his new staff member, who had just graduated from college. Ted was the National VP for a large financial services firm, and we had gotten to know each other over a number of engagements where I came out to speak to his team. We'd had a lot of great conversations, and as we sat in an Irish pub off of Times Square, we had an in-depth conversation about healthcare reform. It was a well-reasoned and respectful discussion between two people who definitely had different opinions. And at the end of the evening, Ted looked at his new hire and said, "This was a great conversation. You might think that I like D. Fish less, but I like him even more because we didn't attack each other. We were each able to share our own perspective. To be successful in business, you have to be able to work and learn from everyone, especially those who are different than you."

I continued to do a lot of work with Ted and his organization, and I still consider him a good friend. I share this as an example of how profersonalism works when it works well. But understand that Ted and I had created a strong foundation for our relationship that formed over time. We had put in the effort to make sure that we trusted and respected each other. There are no shortcuts for that. And if you ever wonder if you should dive deeper into a topic—don't. There will be other opportunities down the line to dig in with your networking partners.

As you build your network, not everyone is going to play well with each other. Some people just don't jive or maybe they have different opinions and don't have the skills to get along with people who are different from them. Don't let this detract from your network, but be aware that you can't just throw everyone in a pot together to see what happens.

When I introduce people to each other, I follow a few internal rules. The first is that I always make introductions with good intentions. I must genuinely think that both people will benefit from the relationship. I treat them as adults, meaning that whether they pursue that connection and whether they "jive" is up to them, and it won't change my opinion of them. I try to give them an "out" as well, so they can save face if things don't work out.

How will you navigate in this world without the comfortable boundaries of our existing social circles? That's a question you have to answer for yourself. In fact, we're trying to figure that out as a society, as well. I think something can be learned by watching married couples who work together professionally. They have the same relationship with each other, no matter the environment, but the way they interact with each other and where they focus their attention varies, depending on the situation. They don't talk about Thanksgiving dinner while they are in a client meeting, and hopefully they take a break from business talk when they are on vacation. But every couple has to negotiate this process for themselves. I think that's what we have to do in our networks, too. It will take more effort because it takes some time to learn how to do it. But it will ultimately be more rewarding. On a personal level, we can have deeper and more authentic relationships, and on a professional level, we will find previously hidden opportunities and be able to get more done with less effort. That sounds like a pretty good payoff to me!

Section III

TAKING STEPS TO UNSUCK YOUR NETWORK!

Let's Talk Tactics!

n this section, we cover the specific tools, language, and processes you can use to be successful with your networking. If you have read the first two sections of this book, fantastic. But if you haven't, that's okay. I know that sometimes we just want to dive in and start doing. The first two sections of the book were meant to give you the strategic background that makes networking make sense. But as someone who played every Xbox video game I ever owned without reading the instruction manual, it would be hypocritical of me to expect everyone to go step-by-step.

I want you to be able to execute the material in this section as quickly as possible, so you will build your confidence and make professional networking an integral part of your life. Whether you are a CEO, a business owner, a sales person, a recruiter, or a rookie professional, instead of blindly hoping that good things will happen through networking, you will be able to plan for and achieve solid results. Here's what this section includes:

Tactic 1: Understand Networking
Tactic 2: Begin Your Journey
Tactic 3: Accept How Networking Really Works
Tactic 4: Build Relationships the Right Way

Tactic 5: Create a Strategic Plan

Tactic 6: Get Over Fear

Tactic 7: Own Your Unique Value

Tactic 8: Define Your Marketing Niche

Tactic 9: Find Your Networking Opportunities

Tactic 10: Rock the Dreaded Elevator Speech

Tactic 11: Deliver Your Group Introduction

Tactic 12: Start and End Conversations Well

Tactic 13: Remember Names

Tactic 14: Make Your One-on-One Introduction Sizzle

Tactic 15: Adjust Your Body Language

Tactic 16: Build a Conversation by Using the Next Question™

Tactic 17: Ask the Right Questions to Find Opportunities

Tactic 18: Network with the Competition

Tactic 19: Follow Up with New Contacts

Tactic 20: Stay Connected with Centers of Influence

Tactic 21: Connect Social Media with Your "Real-World" Activities

Tactic 22: Deepen Your Business Relationships with LinkedIn

Tactic 23: Communicate Effectively on Twitter

Tactic 24: Dive into a Great Networking "First Date"

Tactic 25: Introduce Your Connections to Each Other

Tactic 26: Leverage Your Relationships (When Appropriate)

Tactic 27: Run Your Own Networking Event

Tactic 28: Read Books for More Ideas

Tactic 1

Understanding Networking

N etworking can mean many different things to many different people. Our simple definition is:

"*Networking* is building a web of relationships with others for mutual support in finding business solutions."

The purpose of networking is to create relationships that are:

1. Long-term—they require nurturing and time
2. Mutually beneficial partnerships—they are win/win

Why should networking be an important part of your career planning, no matter what your career is? Networking creates a base for developing ongoing professional growth, whether you are an entrepreneur who is building a new business or a data analyst who works for a large corporation.

1. Networking is relatively inexpensive. For the price of a few coffees and event fees, you can find new opportunities on a regular basis.

2. Networking is a lot of fun. Humans are social creatures, and we can combine our desire for personal relationships with our career needs.

3. Networking is rewarding and supportive. It feels good to find ways to support the people in your network, and they feel the same about helping you.

Whether or not you actually sell a product or service, you are always selling the services of You, Inc. to clients, prospects, peers, employers, and partners. And like any other marketing tool, you need to bring a few pieces together to make your networking work. It requires:

1. Planning – If you approach your networking haphazardly, you will get haphazard results. You need clear and concrete goals and well-defined activities to achieve those goals.

2. Time – The results from networking won't show up overnight. Building a robust network requires a long-term vision and enough space in your calendar in the short-term.

3. Focus – It's easy to get distracted by the noise of your daily responsibilities. Networking doesn't require all of your attention, but you need to give it some focus, or you won't see any benefits.

4. Energy – The magic ingredient for networking success is the energy you bring to it. The value of your network is directly tied to the quality of your relationships, and relationships thrive when there is energy, enthusiasm, and excitement.

With an ever-increasing number of relationships, the effects of your networking activities will continue to grow. The more people you have in your network, the stronger it becomes and the more opportunities you have to help others—and to have others help you.

Tactic 2

Begin Your Journey

T he best time to start networking is now. You might not see an immediate purpose for your network, but why not dig your well before you are thirsty? You might be in a job you love and have all of the resources that you need. That's great, but the business world is fluid and ever-changing. Your future situation might be very different than it is now.

People often struggle with networking because they wait until they need something—and need something fast—to begin. Building relationships naturally takes time. If you only dive into networking when you are actively looking for something, like a new job or more clients, you will end up behind the eight ball. You will miss out on good opportunities because you didn't invest in the relationships, and people can smell desperation. You can rarely shortcut the process and still be successful.

Luckily, you don't have to wait for a specific reason to start networking today. It's perfectly fine to reach out to people even if you don't have a goal in mind. In fact, it can be much more effective to go into networking efforts without a motive because that means you can focus on helping other people. Then they'll be ready and willing to help you when you need support. The first goal is to develop and strengthen your relationships with the people in your network.

Tactic 3

Accept How Networking Really Works

Successful networkers know that networking is often a long play. They don't ignore immediate opportunities, but they also look to create benefit in the future. A short-term focus doesn't work well because it causes you to approach your networking efforts with the wrong lens. The right perspective allows you to take a long-term view that will lead to more success and less stress.

People wish that networking worked like this:
Scenario A

1. You go to a networking event, like a conference or professional mixer.
2. You meet a potential client or employer at the event, and they say they want to work with you.
3. You call them the next day and seal the deal.

But it usually works like this:
Scenario B

1. You go to a formal networking or casual social event.
2. You meet an interesting person, maybe a potential client, employer, or center of influence.
3. You send them a follow-up email after the event.
4. You set up a coffee meeting with them.
5. You send them a post-meeting follow-up email.
6. You go to another networking event and reconnect with them.
7. You send them an email to check in.
8. You go to another networking event and reconnect with them.
9. They suggest you meet one of their contacts.
10. You grab a cup of coffee with that connection.
11. You go to another networking event and reconnect.
12. They tell you about a situation where you can help.
13. You send them an email to set up a meeting about their need.
14. You have a chance to work together.

If you have initial frustrations about the results from your networking activity, keep this in mind: A farmer doesn't expect to harvest a crop the day after the seeds are planted, and relationships take time to grow and bear fruit.

Tactic 4

Build Relationships the Right Way

One of the most important steps in building a robust network is establishing successful relationships. That's why people who take the short-term view usually fail. You can't build relationships by taking shortcuts. Just as your personal relationships take time to nurture and grow, so do your professional relationships.

It will take time to build connections with other people, but you can accelerate the process by making your interactions more meaningful. There is an old sales adage that says, "People do business with people they know, like, and trust." These are good guidelines for building your professional relationships, so focus on these in every conversation.

Know—For your network to be an effective source of business, people have to know who you are. You have to be top-of-mind when they think about your field or industry. Make sure your network knows how you help your clients and customers. When they have a need or a referral in your area of expertise, you should be the first one that comes to mind. Tell people about the kind of projects you like and the clients you've worked with in the past.

Like—How do you make someone like you? It's not about pandering to them or being inauthentic. The easiest way to get people to like you is to find areas where you share an interest. We all like people who are similar us, so find the common ground. And it never hurts to seek out reasons to like them. The more you like someone, the more you will help them, which builds the relationship even further.

Trust—The best way to develop trust is to keep the other person's best interests in mind. Focus on finding win/win scenarios, and always follow through on what you say you'll do. Build trust in your professional relationships in the same way you build trust in your personal relationships—by being trustworthy and dependable. Trust is earned, not given.

Tactic 5

Create a Strategic Plan

Many people network with loosely or completely undefined goals. Because they don't know what they are aiming for, they don't recognize the most valuable activities and usually get inconsistent results. When you have a plan in place before you start networking, it makes your networking easier and more effective. Take time to write down answers to the following questions before you start your networking.

1. Who do I want to meet?
   - Do you want to meet clients or potential employers?
   - Do you want to meet vendors or suppliers for your business?
   - Do you want to meet referral partners, i.e., people that will refer business to you?

2. What business results are you seeking?
   - Look at your overall business goals, and decide how networking will fit in.
   - What kind of professionals should be in your network?
   - Are there secondary benefits you can achieve as well?

3. What activities will create these results?
   - How much activity do you need to create the results you want?
   - Where should you spend your networking time and attention?
   - Can you invest the time and energy up front to get the results you want?

Tactic 6

Get Over Fear

When we put ourselves out there professionally, it requires concentrated effort and can be intimidating. For example, when you go to a networking event where you don't know anyone else, it feels exactly like going to a party where you don't know anyone—it's stressful. No matter how confident you are, it's easy to wonder, "Will they like me?" or "Will I have anything to say?" or worse, "Wouldn't it be easier to just stay home?"

Our main obstacles are often these negative internal questions. Our own inner fears can stop us before we even get started because starting new relationships, even professional ones, can be a daunting task. Learning to conquer this fear can be a big part of a successful networking plan.

Here's how you can get over the negative chatter in your mind:

1. Remember the value of networking. It may feel intimidating to walk into a room of strangers or to call someone on the phone to set up a coffee meeting, but remember how it will benefit your business when you build these relationships.

2. Understand that others are nervous, too. If you are uncomfortable reaching out to new people, it helps to know that they have similar feelings. That person who is standing alone at a networking event is rarely aloof; they are nervous, too. They'll appreciate it if you take the first step.

3. Take someone with you. There's nothing wrong with having some support. Call a colleague or friend and ask them to go to the event with you, or have a small coffee meeting with two or three other people to spread out the conversation. It's easier to mingle when you know at least one other person, and your friend will make some good connections too.

Tactic 7

Own Your Unique Value

O ne of the biggest challenges we have is how to make our message "sticky." Do people remember you and the services you provide? You can create a lasting impression when you share what makes you unique. The more you communicate what sets you apart from others, the easier it is for your new connections to know what you do and to recommend you.

There are four areas where you can differentiate yourself and your business:

1. Your mission—why do you work with your customers?
2. Your method—how do you work with your customers?
3. The demographics—who are your customers?
4. Your service—what do you do for them?

When we are trying to solve a problem, we want to deal with people who are experts in their field. We want someone who knows how to handle our specific situation. Because there are so many variables in every field and industry, it will help your prospects if you define your specialized niche. If you try to be everything to everybody, you'll end up being nothing to nobody.

Define Your Marketing Niche

Establishing a marketing niche is important for all businesses, including You, Inc. One of the easiest ways to set yourself apart is to clearly define your unique marketing niche. If you are a salesperson or business owner, you want to define your ideal customers. If you are a service provider, you want to define the specific situations where you excel. If you are looking for your next job, you want to define exact problems you can solve for an employer.

That is how you can make yourself unique as a professional. You differentiate yourself in terms of your client base and who you serve and what makes them unique, such as:

- Their location
- Their industry or profession
- Their business or consumer focus
- The size of their company
- Their income or revenue bracket
- Their personal demographics (age, education, etc.)

Why have a marketing niche?

1. It's a way to communicate about your ideal customer/business partner. People can only refer you to others if they know exactly what kind of connection you seek. When you have planted a flag in their mind, they are more likely to remember you.
2. It focuses your thinking and your efforts. Instead of scattering your energy everywhere, you can focus it on building the right relationships with people who either are, or can refer you to, your ideal contact.
3. It positions you to become the expert in your field. When you define yourself as somebody who works with a particular type of client, it sticks in people's minds. You want be the first person that pops into their head when they think of your industry or profession.

It's important to remember that a marketing niche isn't exclusionary. You can still work with people who don't fit that mold if they come to you. The key word here is "marketing." It's a way to tell others what type of contacts you are looking for in a manner they can grasp. Never assume that people know what you are looking for from your network. You think about your business all of the time—they don't. Make it easy for them to understand.

Tactic 9

Find Your Networking Opportunities

You can network anywhere you are. There are no special circumstances that are needed so you can always be networking. Whether it's breakfast with a formal networking group or a spontaneous opportunity at the grocery store, you should always be ready to build relationships as you go about your day. Structured networking events, where people are specifically focused on meeting new professionals, are a great place to add new blood to your existing network. And it can be just as valuable to bring people from your personal world into your professional circles.

As you make explicit plans to create business through networking, it helps to determine a few specific venues where those relationships can start.

Places that you can network:

1. Informal
   - Church groups
   - Volunteer organizations
   - Civic organizations

- Clubs and hobby groups
- Sports teams and gyms

2. Structured
   - Chambers of Commerce
   - Trade associations
   - Formal lead groups: BNI, LeTip, Leads Club, etc.
   - Local business organizations
   - Start your own!

Three criteria to make sure it's the right group for you:

1. There must be the right type of contacts for you. Every group is not created equal. Different types of professionals will congregate in a variety of organizations. In fact, the same group in different cities can have a very different demographic. Look for alignment between your goals and the participants.

2. You must like the people involved. Effective networking is built on relationships, and it's a lot easier to build relationships with people that you enjoy. Just as every group attracts different participants, each group also has a different vibe. Find ones that include people you want to connect with. Just because it is net*working,* that doesn't mean it can't be fun!

3. You must feel you can contribute something. If you feel outclassed or intimidated by the group, you aren't going to feel comfortable reaching out to the individual members. Likewise, if you can only take and not give, it is going to feel "off "—and that's bad karma. Put yourself in situations where you can give back, as well as gain. Perhaps you can give referrals, expertise, or offer to connect your contacts, but make sure you pull your own weight.

Tactic 10

Rock the Dreaded Elevator Speech

The first impression you give of you and your business is usually your introduction or elevator speech. Most formal networking events have a time where each person has between 30 to 60 seconds to introduce themselves and their business to the entire group. Take the time to create a simple but powerful introduction that starts those relationships off strong.

Three Guidelines for Introductions

1. Keep it short. Almost every elevator speech is too long. There's a reason it's called an elevator speech—it's supposed to be short. If you're in an elevator with the perfect contact and have only a few floors to convey what you do, what will you say to leave a strong impression? This isn't a sales pitch, and you don't have to mention everything. It's an introduction. Capture their interest, and make them want to know more. And then stop talking.

2. Keep it simple. You live in your brain. You think about what you do 24 hours a day, 7 days a week. There are layers of

nuance and tons of assumptions in your mind. Keep in mind that your audience doesn't know any of that. Make everything as simple as possible. If you think "this is so obvious" to yourself while you are giving your introduction, you are on the right track. Easy to understand = easy to remember. And that's what you want.

3. Keep it relevant. Even though your audience is listening to you talk about you, human nature says that your audience is still thinking about themselves and their own problems. You aren't going to change human nature, so make sure that what you share is relevant to the audience. Tell them how your professional experiences and skills can help them solve their problems.

The Structure of a Great Introduction

1. Tell your name, title (what you do), and company.
2. Tell them your mission (or your tag).
   a. Come up with something consistent (brand yourself).
   b. It doesn't have to be funny or clever to be successful.
   c. This is your hook—just like a song—so find your refrain and repeat it.

3. Give them a relevant piece of information (pick one—this can/should change).
   a. Here's a fact you might not have known.
   b. Here's the ideal referral for me that you might not have thought about.
   c. Here's an important industry fact that has changed.
   d. Here's a new product or service that we offer.

    e. Here's a twist on a current product or service that you might not know.

4. Give them a reason/way to act now.
    a. Talk to me afterwards:
       i. If you know someone who could use this service
      ii. If you want a consultation
     iii. If you have any questions
    b. Follow me on (insert social media platform) at _____.
    c. See my website, which is _____.

5. Repeat your name, title (what you do), and company.

Here's what I say:

> "Hi, I'm David Fisher, but everyone calls me D. Fish. I'm the president of RockStar Consulting, a professional development company that helps people become RockStars in their professional lives. We offer 1:1 business coaching, skill development workshops, and keynote speaking services. I recently released my first full-length book, which I'm pretty proud of. It's called *Networking in the 21st Century: Why Your Network Sucks and What to Do About It*. If you or if someone you know wants to get better at networking, please introduce yourself. Again, my name is D. Fish, and I'm the president of RockStar Consulting."

Tactic 11

Deliver Your Group Introduction

Once you have the words down, you have to focus on your delivery. Communication is much more than what you say; it's also how you say it. Getting everyone to hear and understand your introduction can be especially challenging in chaotic environments like large professional events. Use all of the tools at your disposal to ensure that you are projecting the message you want.

Make sure everyone can see your face. When you sit in the middle of a room, there's a good chance that when you stand up, you will have your back to some of your audience. No matter how many lunges you've been doing at the gym lately, it's never good to shut someone out and make them listen to your back. The fix is easy. When it's your turn to speak, simply stand up and walk to the edge of the room, and turn so everyone can see you. They'll be able to hear you better and see your facial expressions, which are both important communication tools.

Project your voice so that everyone can hear you. It sounds obvious, but if they can't hear you, your audience can't know you. This usually means you will be speaking louder than you normally do—that's okay. You have to make sure that those who are the farthest away can still hear everything you say. This is especially important if you have a naturally soft voice or one that is difficult to understand from a distance. For example, deep voices carry farther, but they tend to distort, so speak up, speak clearly, and leave the Barry White impression for later.

Stand tall and smile. What if you had to introduce yourself, but you couldn't speak? What would you do? A very small percent of what we communicate comes through our words, so you might be able to get away with it. (Not that I'm suggesting being mute at your next meeting.) The best thing to do when you introduce yourself is to stand up straight, which shows that you are confident, and smile, which shows you are open and friendly. Let your body language do some of the talking for you.

How to Start and End Conversations

When engaging with strangers, the beginning and ending of conversations can feel intimidating. Instead of figuring out complex and difficult ways to start a conversation, keep it simple. You can also find members of the group who know most of the others—many groups even have ambassadors to assist new members—and ask them to introduce you.

How to enter a conversation:

"Hi, my name is _____, what's yours?

"Hi, my name is _____, how are you enjoying the event?

"I'm sorry to interrupt, but I just wanted to introduce myself."

How to leave the conversation:

"It has been great meeting you, but I know we're both here to meet a lot of new people. I've enjoyed our conversation, let's be sure to follow up with each other."

It's that simple.

Tactic 13

Remember Names

One of the greatest concerns about networking is that we often are afraid we won't remember the other person's name. It's embarrassing to meet someone, and then forget their name the next time you see them.

Don't let this curtail your networking efforts. There are many different tricks and memory devices to help you remember names; you just need to find the one that works for you. For example, I often ask someone who has an unusual name to spell it for me. And while they spell it, I visualize a typewriter typing it out. This works for me because I'm a visual learner. I also ask people who have common names that could be spelled a variety of ways (Eric/Erik, Susie/Suzy, Chris/Kris) if they would spell it for me. They appreciate that because they're tired of having their name misspelled, and I get the chance to spell it out in my head.

That could work for you too, or it could be a complete bust. You might have a visual memory like me, or you might remember better through auditory information or word associations. Because we all learn different ways, there is no single, foolproof way to remember names. Test the following methods and use the one that works for you:

10 Ways to Remember Names:

1. Never say or think to yourself, "I'm bad with names."
2. Always be mentally present when introductions are made.
3. Look at the person's face while you repeat their name to yourself.
4. Attach a mental image to their name.
5. Ask them to spell their name.
6. Write something down afterwards that you can associate with them.
7. Use their name immediately.
8. Repeat their name to yourself three times (internally).
9. Associate a fact, phrase, or word with their name.
10. Introduce the person to someone else.

If you do forget someone's name, don't make it a big deal. Just say, "I'm sorry, I can't recall your name. Can you help me out?" There's a good chance they've forgotten yours, too!

Make Your One-on-One Introduction Sizzle

When you meet someone for the first time, you could easily introduce yourself in a manner that is interesting to you, but not to them. When you introduce yourself, you want that introduction to be more about them than it is about you. You want to engage them from the very beginning.

1. Don't talk about what you do, tell them what you provide.
2. Don't list the features of your work, let them know the benefits to those you serve.
3. Instead of talking about yourself, talk about them.

The goal is to make a solid impression the first time you have a one-on-one conversation. This doesn't replace your elevator speech introduction; it's only for when you meet someone individually for the first time.

Practice until you find a leading sentence that's engaging. For example, if you were an insurance agent and said, "I sell insurance," it wouldn't draw the other person in. But if you said, "I help people protect the things and people that are most important to them so they can focus on the best parts of life," that could lead to a much more interesting conversation.

- "I help people make their dream home a reality home." Real Estate Agent
- "I help align people's financial goals with their life goals." Financial Planner
- "I make sure that people can always find their keys." Professional Organizer
- "I help people sleep at night." Security System Provider
- "I bring people's ideas to life on the page." Graphic Designer
- "I protect people from making the same mistakes as Al Capone." Accountant

Tactic 15

Adjust Your Body Language

W hen having a conversation, how you present yourself is just as important as what you say. How you carry yourself is critical because most of our communication comes through our body language and facial expressions. Using non-verbal cues can be a fantastic way to create stronger relationships—if you know what you are doing. Here are few simple places to start.

1. Stand up straight! Most of us have poor posture because we sit in front of a computer all day and hunch our shoulders when we type. (If you don't believe me, pull your shoulder blades back and see what opens up.) This causes us to slouch and shrink downward, which is definitely not the way to project confidence. Before you walk into a meeting, stand with your feet hip-width apart, pretend that there is a string attached to the very top of your head, and then imagine that someone is pulling that string upward. You'll notice a difference in your posture right away.

2. Smile! We like people who are friendly, and one of the easiest ways to show friendliness is with a smile. Even blind people

who have never seen a face will smile when they are happy. The key is to make your smiling unconscious instead of a deliberate activity that needs your attention. You can do this by creating a good mood that influences you for the rest of the conversation. Think of something that makes you happy (like puppies or kittens or your children) before you have an important conversation, and you'll be more likely to smile during the meeting. You don't have to tell anyone what you are doing, but it will shift your internal attitude.

3. Lean in. Leaning in is useful on both a metaphoric and practical level. When you lean in to the conversation, you show interest. When two people are physically aligned in a conversation, it says volumes about their levels of engagement. You've seen it yourself in restaurants; you can tell if a couple is on a date and how it's going by the way they are sitting. Definitely don't lean back. That indicates disengagement.

4. Orient your body. We show we are interested in others when we turn our body toward them. When you meet someone new or if someone else joins a conversation in progress, adjust your body to include them. Don't turn your back on anyone. And if you are standing, point your feet toward them a little. It's a small thing, but it will bring them into the conversation more fully.

Build a Conversation by Using the Next Question™

I t can be intimidating to be in a room full of strangers, but if you can turn those strangers into friends, it can be an exciting opportunity. Asking questions is a powerful way to establish rapport with someone and to create the foundation for a relationship. The Next Question™ is an easy method for using questions and answers to stimulate a conversation.

This is how you naturally engage with friends and family. When you ask your significant other about their day, you're using this Next Question™ format. Since you already use this technique with people you know, it's a simple shift it to use with someone you just met.

Simply use the answers that your conversational partner provides as the basis for the next question you ask. Keep the conversation focused on them for a while, instead of using their answers as a way to turn the conversation back to you. Avoid questions that have yes/no answers because they tend to kill the conversation.

Use basic questions to get the conversation rolling:

1. How?
2. Why?

3. Where?
4. When?
5. How long/often?

In a conversation with a real estate agent:

How long have you been in real estate?

9 Years.

You must have gotten the hang of it! Where do you sell most of your houses?

I mostly work in the Uptown area.

What do you like about working around there?

The area has a lot of young families buying their first homes, and I like working with them.

That's very cool. What's the best part about working with them?

-or-

In a conversation with an entrepreneur:

Why did you decide to start you own business?

I really like being able to create my own destiny. I like to be responsible for my future.

That sounds interesting and intense. What has been the hardest thing about running a start-up?

It's great because every day is different, but that also means that there isn't a lot of stability.

I can imagine. But there must be a lot of excitement, too. What's the biggest project you are working on right now?

-or-

In a conversation at a holiday party in your neighborhood:

How did you come to live around here?

My wife got a job here in town.
Oh, where were you before?
We were actually in New York.
Did you both grow up there?
Actually, my wife did, but I'm from the Netherlands.
Really, that's awesome. What brought you to the U.S.?

To build rapport with others, you need to find connections and commonalities. The Next Question™ allows you to do so. When it's appropriate, you can share tidbits about yourself as well. In the scenario above, for example, perhaps you also spent time in New York. You could share that as a way to build a bridge. But don't hijack the conversation. Share something about yourself, and then use a question to point the conversation back to the other person.

Tactic 17

Ask the Right Questions to Find Opportunities

O nce you've established a basic rapport, take the time to find out the specifics about their professional world. There are a variety of targeted questions you can ask to find out more about their career and how you can help them. Remember the power of networking karma. It's equally important to find ways to help others as it is to tell others how they can help you.

You want to discover how you can help them:

1. Develop their career. Almost everyone you meet wants to build their career, just like you want to build yours. There are often simple ways that you can support your connections in their professional growth, but you need to uncover those opportunities before you can offer help.

2. Solve professional problems. All professionals have problems. Whether they're big or small, we all need to move past obstacles and solve challenges. You might have an insight or experience you can share with your connection, once you understand the obstacles they have.

3. Create partnerships. One of the rewarding parts of networking is the opportunity to pair two of your contacts together to create a new partnership. It might be a formal relationship, such as connecting a salesperson with a new client, or something more informal, such as pairing two professionals in the same industry to build their own networking relationship. Find out information that allows you to see the links between people.

4. Find referrals. Most people in your network want to make new connections. They might be looking for new clients and customers, or they may be trying to find their next employer. There's a good chance that you can get them one step closer to an ideal introduction, but you have to know what they are looking for first. The more you understand what types of connections they want to make, the more easily you can hook them up with the right person.

Good discovery questions fall into three categories:

1. What is your biggest opportunity?
- How can your business grow right now?
- What obstacle is holding you back?
- What is your biggest challenge?
- What is your biggest headache?
- What is causing you a lot of problems right now?

2. What are your strengths?
- What is your primary service?
- Why do people like to work with you?
- What are you famous for or known for?
- What would your top customers say about you?
- What do you love doing?

3. **How can I help?**
   - Who are your best customers?
   - How can I best explain what you do?
   - What do you look for in a partner?
   - Who are you looking to meet?
   - How have people in my position served you before?

Tactic 18

Network with the Competition

People often wonder how they are supposed to network when there are competitors in the room. What do you do when someone in your network is also in your line of work? Should you ignore them? Talk about them behind their back?

Don't panic. Rather than viewing them as the enemy, look for ways you can help each other. Look at your professional world as a collaborative effort instead of a zero-sum game. There is more than enough business to go around.

Don't see them as competitors, but as colleagues. If you can find ways to co-exist, there's a good chance that both of your businesses can improve. The saying goes, "A rising tide raises all ships." Instead of looking for ways to sink their proverbial ship, look for ways you can support each other.

1. Focus on common goals. Unless your goal is to drive your competition out of business, you probably have similar goals. You both want to build your business, take care of your customers, make a good living, etc.

2. Discuss mutual areas of opportunity. Find ways that you can team up to build both of your businesses. There are often projects that you couldn't do alone that would work well if you partnered with another professional.

3. Share challenges. Nobody wants to hang around people who are always negative, but who is going to understand your challenges better than someone who does the same thing you do? You don't have to share weaknesses that they could exploit, but they might have some ideas on ways to solve your problems, just like you might be able to help them.

4. Define and refine your ideal clients. This is where having a clear focus is important. Even though your competitor might be in the same industry, an in-depth discussion will often reveal that you each have a different focus in your business. You might even be able to refer business to each other when you have a prospect that needs something you can't provide.

Tactic 19

Follow Up with New Contacts

You met someone to add to your network. Now what? You can easily lose the benefits of networking if you don't have adequate follow-up. This is a huge mistake. Our goal is to build relationships. And how many of your relationships are based on meeting someone just one time? Before you start building your network, you should plan how you will to follow up with everyone you meet and how you will nurture these new relationships.

1. Keep a database of the people you meet, and enter new contacts into it as soon as possible.
   - Spend 5 to 15 minutes after each event to organize your business cards
     i. Put them in a box, rubber-band them together, or use Outlook or a CRM. Organize them:
        1. Alphabetically
        2. By industry
        3. By customer/vendor/partner
        4. By who you will follow up with
        5. By business card color (that's a joke)

2. Send a quick email or note to the people you met at the event. If it was an informal encounter, you can still send a quick "it was nice to meet you" note.
   - Most people don't do this
   - You'll make an impression and stand out in their mind

3. Follow up with the best contacts as soon as possible with:
   - An offer for a follow-up phone chat
   - An offer for a follow-up meeting—lunch or coffee
   - An introduction to another possible connection
   - An article or blog post that might be relevant to them

Take the time to follow up. It's something that will set you apart from the rest. Great networkers do what other people don't.

Tactic 20

Stay Connected with Centers of Influence

As your network develops, you'll find you have a short list of professionals who drive most of the referrals and opportunities to you. They are often people who are at the center of their own vibrant networks. These centers of influence connect to many professionals and have the ability to leverage their relationships. It can be even better when they love what you do and love to tell people about you—when they become your champions. It can be easy to meet these people in the course of your networking because they are big networkers themselves.

How do you stay on the top of their referral list?

1. Attend the events they attend.
   You can't replace the power of face-to-face interaction. That doesn't mean you have to grab lunch with them every week, however. Continue to attend group networking events, even after you've started a relationship, so that you can put in a few minutes of face time with your most important connections. It can be useful to see and be seen at events.

2. Use social media.

   Be sure to connect with your centers of influence and champions on social media, whether it's LinkedIn, Twitter, or Facebook. Monitor what they say and post regularly yourself. Listen and chime in when you can add something useful to the conversation. Social media gives you the opportunity to have low-effort conversations in the background of your daily activities.

3. Send regular emails or e-newsletters.

   It's worth putting forth a little effort to move beyond a background conversation every now and then. If you have an e-newsletter you send out, that's perfect. If not, get in the habit of sending out a brief status update every month or so.

4. Join their distribution lists.

   Getting on their distribution list is just as important as sending out your own newsletters. Even if you only glance at their e-newsletters and emails, it will keep you informed about what they're doing. And it makes them feel good that people read their messages, just like you feel good when people read yours.

5. Introduce them to new people.

   Always be on the lookout for new connections you can create. Centers of influence are, by definition, at the center of a networking web, and they are always looking for new connections. If you know someone you think they should know, send a quick introductory email, and tell them why they should meet. There's a reason they have a robust network; they like to meet people and will be grateful for new introductions.

Connect Social Media with Your "Real-World" Activities

Social media is one of the biggest game changers to hit the networking landscape in recent years. It's a key ingredient to bring your networking into the 21st century, but that doesn't mean it will replace all of your offline networking. When you use social media correctly, it becomes a communication tool that helps you build relationships more quickly and stay in touch with a wider group of connections.

- Before you dive into social media, ask yourself these three questions:
    1. What are my most important business goals? (attract more clients, find a new job, get a promotion, etc.)
    2. Who is the most important audience for me to communicate with to accomplish that goal?
    3. What message does that audience need to hear from me?
- Integrate social media into your offline networking. The goal isn't to have purely virtual networking partners, although that will happen and it can be very useful. Rather, use social media

to create more powerful offline relationships. Look for ways you can use it to stay in touch with your extended network.

- You should embrace social media as a powerful communication tool. You shouldn't try to master every social media site. It takes time and attention to leverage any platform, and if you try to spread yourself too thin, you'll be ineffective, or you'll spend all your time online and none of it will go toward accomplishing your business goals.

- There isn't a one-size-fits-all mix of social media sites for professional networking. It will vary depending on your industry and your professional goals. The most effective strategy is to match your goals with the platform. Each platform provides something different. For example,

  o Most professionals start with **LinkedIn**, the pre-eminent business-oriented social media platform. It's no longer just a site for people looking for a new job, although it's great for that. No matter what your networking goals are, LinkedIn should be a cornerstone of your online activity.

  o **Twitter** can be useful if you are in an industry that has a lot of high-velocity information, meaning information that's relevant right now. For example, journalists, event planners, and recruiters are all frequent users of Twitter. It can also be useful for building your personal brand if you are a thought leader. However, it has a steep learning curve to become effective, so be prepared to put in some work up front.

  o Your professional network will already be partially on **Facebook** if you are creating a Profersonal™ network (see Chapter 11). That being said, there are often more problems with privacy and security that can be created on Facebook than can be solved. Unless you are really comfortable with the etiquette involved in integrating your professional and personal networks, I'd skip this as a main focus.

- ○ Other sites like **YouTube, Instagram, Pinterest, Blogs,** and **Tumblr** can be very useful. Remember to align the sites you use with your goals before you invest your time and energy in them.

- Most sites give you the ability to create an easy-to-find public profile. Don't rush through this step. This is a passive brand message that is available to your network 24/7. For example, depending on how common your name is in your area and industry, if someone looks you up by name and location on Google, there is a good chance that your LinkedIn profile will be one of the top results. You never know when someone will look for information about you, so make sure you are sharing the message you want the public to see.

- Create systems and processes so that you don't spend all your time on social media. For example, spending ten minutes in the morning looking at your newsfeeds to monitor your network is much more efficient than checking it throughout the day. You can also use platforms like Hootsuite and Buffer to manage your social media posts. It's easier to write and post once a week instead of constantly searching for content to post.

Tactic 22

Deepen Your Business Relationships with LinkedIn

While online networking won't replace the power of meeting people face-to-face, LinkedIn provides a powerful tool to follow up and stay connected with the network you are building.

- Create an optimized profile. Your LinkedIn profile is your personal professional website. It's always available to your network, and you want to make sure you communicate the message you want to share. Here are three important places to put your focus:
  - Profile photo. Make sure your photo is polished and approachable, and choose one that is consistent with the message on the rest of your profile.
  - Headline. Found right below your name, the headline functions just like a newspaper article headline. It attracts attention and sets the tone for the rest of the profile.
  - Summary. This is where you talk to your audience. Imagine the perfect business contact was sitting across the table from you. What would you say?

- Invite people to connect with you. LinkedIn is the perfect tool for maintaining relationships with your weak connections. When you meet someone at a networking function, follow up with an invitation to connect on LinkedIn. Many of them will accept, and you now have a chance to engage with them over time. In the same way, you can stay in touch with colleagues from past companies and old classmates in just a few minutes a day.

- Research your networking partners. When you fill out your profile, you share the most important information about you as a professional. Your contacts do the same thing when they complete their profiles. Before you go into a meeting with someone, take a few moments to go through their profile. You'll find intriguing areas to ask about, such as previous jobs or volunteer organizations. You'll also find common areas of interest, such as going to the same school or even shared connections. You can then dive into relevant conversations immediately instead of waiting to stumble onto them.

- Don't ignore the wealth of information contained in the newsfeed. It's easy to simply share your content on LinkedIn, but you must also "listen" to what others say. When people share updates, pay attention. Not all of them will be relevant, but when they are, be sure to respond. This is how you can keep your finger on the pulse of your network with little effort, and it's one of LinkedIn's most useful benefits.

- Use the "Status Update" feature. You can share articles, photos, videos, and other information through status updates. The two components to building your brand with your network are visibility and reputation. Do people see you? What do they associate with you when they do? Post current information about what's happening in your business world to keep your network informed of what you are working on and how you can help them.

- Give and ask for recommendations and endorsements. Credibility is the currency of online networking, and recommendations and endorsements help establish that credibility. Recommendations are great for people you've worked with closely—colleagues, direct reports, clients, service providers, etc. If you don't have a strong relationship with a connection but know that they excel at what they do, endorse two or three of their skills.

- Join groups. Groups are one of LinkedIn's most powerful features. Use them to connect with people who have the same interests as you, whether you share a profession, a hobby, or an alma mater. It's a great way to uncover new opportunities and build your network in ways that might not be possible offline.

Tactic 23

Communicate Effectively on Twitter

Using Twitter tends to make people nervous, especially those who don't normally use it. Many professionals regard it as the penultimate social media tool. Unlike sites such as LinkedIn that revolve around your profile, Twitter focuses on sharing information through the lens of 140-character status updates.

Do you have to use Twitter to be an effective networker? Of course not. But it can be incredibly useful, especially if you want to build your network beyond your geographical area. Think of Twitter as a networking event that has 200 million+ professionals in attendance, which means there are a number of inherent challenges and opportunities. It's noisy, it's full of irrelevant information, and there can be a steep learning curve. The upside is that the perfect contact may be sitting out there just waiting for you to reach out.

This is an oversimplification, of course, but if you want to use Twitter for networking, here are a few ideas to save you time and energy:

- Listen more than you share, especially in the beginning. Twitter is a great place to lurk. Find out what your connections are sharing, and stay in the know. It's a wonderful place to stay informed about what is happening in your industry.

- Create an effective Twitter bio. While not nearly as robust as other online profiles, your Twitter bio is important because it follows you around. Anytime someone sees one of your posts, the 160 characters of your bio are just a click away. Take the time to ensure that those 160 characters reflect who you are.

- Use lists to organize the people you follow. As I said, Twitter is a loud and crazy party. As you follow more and more professionals, your Twitter feed will become unmanageable. Use the lists feature to separate your Twitter connections into easily digestible groups. I suggest you put people in groups according to their field or industry and how they relate to you. I have a blogger list, and I also have a "friends from Chicago" list.

- When you are ready to engage in conversation, learn the shorthand for the site. Do you know how to use a direct reply vs. a mention vs. a retweet? Understand the shortcuts the system uses that allow you to engage with other users. And we haven't even talked about hashtags yet, which are another way to organize Twitter conversations. The best way to get the latest information on Twitter communication and etiquette is a quick Google search of "twitter beginner guide."

Keep your use in concert with your networking and business goals. Your Twitter feed can be like a slot machine because it gives you little shots of dopamine every time a new post comes up—and you don't even have to put in any money. It can be addicting. Don't get lost in the social media maze. Always remember what you want to accomplish.

Tactic 24

Dive into a Great Networking "First Date"

Many of us get frustrated by networking because we find it difficult to create meaningful business relationships where both parties know each other and want to help. You can get stuck in a never-ending cycle of large networking events, getting buried in business cards but never getting results.

You can break that pattern and move past the stand-in-a-room-full-of-strangers situation. Invite some of the professionals you meet at these events to have a cup of coffee. It's practically impossible to get to know someone in a big, crowded room, but it's pretty simple when you have a conversation at your local coffeehouse. You don't have to invite everyone you meet. Just reach out to the people with whom you think you could create a mutually beneficial connection or those you simply enjoyed meeting.

The next step is to have a really good conversation over that cup of coffee. Think of it as a first date for business. Ask genuinely sincere questions so that you can learn about that person, their business, and how you can help them. As you ask questions, they will usually reciprocate and find out more about you in return. When you ask insightful questions, you'll find that you have many similarities with your networking partner, and you'll find ways to help each other professionally.

Take a look at the starter questions below, but don't feel like you have to go straight down the list and ask question after question. Just use them as a guide or to prompt the conversation. The more you know about them and their business, the better your professional relationship will be.

1. Where are you from?
2. Where did you go to school?
3. What is your degree in?
4. How long have you lived where you live?
5. What do you like about living there?
6. Why did you choose your current career?
7. What did you do before this position?
8. What do you like best about what you do?
9. What do you like least about what you do?
10. Where do you see your career in five years?
11. Why do you do what you do?
12. What are your favorite types of people to work with?
13. What's the best quality of your company?
14. What is unique about your company and how you work?
15. What is your biggest obstacle in the next year?
16. What is your biggest business opportunity this year?
17. What other organizations are you involved in?
18. What do you like about them?
19. What are your favorite hobbies?
20. What do you think of people in my line of work?

Tactic 25

Introduce Your Connections to Each Other

Making connections is great, but don't throw two of your contacts together without setting them up for success. It's important to make sure that both parties have a clear path forward when making introductions. Of course, make sure the two parties have the correct contact information. They will also want to know the context of the relationship in order to benefit from their conversation. Email introductions are the easiest way to connect them. Be sure your message includes:

- Why you are making the referral.
- How you know the referred.
- That you are carbon copying the referred on the email.
- The next action step.

Here are some examples:

Hi John,

I wanted to follow up on our conversation the other day. You said you were looking to build your business, and

I think working with a business coach like David might be a big help. I met David through a networking group, and I've had the chance to use his services. He really helped me out. You can contact him by phone at ———. I've also cc'd him on this email, so you can contact him at the above email address.

Good Luck!

Lisa

Hi Carlos and Bill,

I wanted to introduce you because I think you would benefit from meeting each other. Carlos is the president of a small plumbing supply company, and I know him from the Chamber of Commerce. Bill is a good friend of mine from college, and he is an expert at helping companies improve their presence online through developing content marketing plans. I think you would enjoy meeting each other.

Carlos, this is Bill.

Bill, meet Carlos.

You can grab each other's email address from the cc. Have fun!

David

And don't forget to tell your network know how to refer people back to you. You can use a version of this email to let them know how to connect you:

Hi Susan,

Thanks for being willing to help me out! Referrals are a huge part of my business. When you know someone that you'd like to refer to me, the best way to do so is to email them my phone number and cc: me on that email. That way we both have each other's contact info, and I can prepare for their phone call. Thanks, I really appreciate it.

Warmest Regards,

David

Tactic 26

Leverage Your Relationships (When Appropriate)

B uilding relationships is fun and rewarding in itself. But this is networking, so you want to leverage those relationships when appropriate. Many professionals are hesitant to do so because they don't want to be perceived as obnoxious or pushy. They also don't know how to ask. If you've built up enough relationship capital with a person, it doesn't have to be awkward

Let the person know what kind of help you need, and why you need it. And be sure to leave them an "out," so they can take a pass on your request without feeling bad. You don't know everything that is going on in your contact's professional life, and they might not be in a position to help you at that particular moment. Here are a few easy scripts you can use:

How to ask for an introduction

"Jim, I think that you know Susan over at Company XYZ. I was looking into a position they have available there, and I was hoping you could introduce us. I'd like to understand what the firm is like from someone who works there and to hopefully get connected with the hiring manager. If you don't know her well enough, no worries. Thanks!"

How to ask for referrals

"I'm currently building my client base and am always on the look-out for new people I can help. Who do you know that I might be able to work with? Do you know anyone who needs my services, particularly people who need _____? If you don't know anyone right now, that's totally okay."

How to ask for business or a meeting

"You mentioned that you were looking to _____ the last time we spoke. I think I might be able to help you with that. Do you have time for a quick meeting next week by phone or over a cup of coffee? Let me know what works best for you. We can also schedule it later down the line if you are too busy right now."

Tactic 27

Run Your Own Networking Event

hese days it seems like networking events are springing up everywhere. No matter where you live or work, you could find a networking breakfast or cocktail reception to attend just about every day of the week. Many of these events brag about how large they are and how many people you can meet if you attend.

There's nothing wrong with going to large events, but many people find them overwhelming, and it can be hard to make good connections in the hustle and bustle of a crowded room. What can you do?

Put together your own networking event.

It's not as hard as it sounds, and it can be very rewarding. Don't be concerned about organizing a huge event. Make it more personal, and get together with five to seven professionals you want to get to know who could also benefit from knowing each other. Here are some simple steps to get you started:

1. Pick a place. It helps if the venue is centrally located and easy to access. Coffeehouses and bars work the best because everyone can buy their own beverage, and there are no additional costs. Restaurants are also nice, but then you have

to worry about paying for food and divvying up the check at the end.

2. Invite people. It's best to invite 10 or 12 contacts; about half of them will be able to attend. Choose people that you want to get to know, but who will want to know each other as well. Consider their jobs and their personalities. It helps, but is not essential, if everyone shares a common type of customer, such as a group of realtors, insurance agents, and mortgage providers.

3. Set a time. The two best times to meet are right before or right after work. You can also meet during the day if you know that all the attendees have a flexible schedule. It doesn't have to last long; even an hour can be enough time to give everyone a chance to chat.

4. Send the invitations. Email is fine, or depending on your industry, you could even use Twitter. You can also give people a quick call. A simple invite works well:

I'd like to invite you to an informal networking event that I'm planning at Joe's Coffeehouse on July 17 from 8:00 to 9:00 a.m. There will be five to ten attendees, and it's a chance to really get to know some great contacts for your professional network. Please RSVP by July 10; I really hope you can make it.

5. Network. The whole point of the event is for people to meet each other and have conversations. Because you're the host and you know everyone—at least by name—introduce each of the attendees to each other. Since it's a small group, there's no need for the formality of name tags. If the group is on the smaller end—around five people—it can be effective

to have a single conversation around the table. If the group is larger, people will naturally want to have their own side conversations.

Ask everyone to pass out their business cards, and encourage them to follow up after the event. Not only will you have made stronger connections with your network, but everyone will appreciate the new contacts they made, thanks to you.

Tactic 28

Read Books for More Ideas

Here are some books I recommend that will further build your networking and communication skills:

- *How To Win Friends and Influence People* by Dale Carnegie
- *To Sell Is Human: The Surprising Truth About Moving Others* by Daniel Pink
- *Drive: The Surprising Truth About What Motivates Us* by Daniel Pink
- *Superconnect: Harnessing the Power of Networks and the Strength of Weak Links* by Richard Koch and Greg Lockwood
- *Super Staying Power: What You Need to Become Valuable and Resilient at Work* by Jason Seiden
- *Endless Referrals: Network Your Everyday Contacts Into Sales* by Bob Burg
- *Never Eat Alone: And Other Secrets to Success, One Relationship at a Time* by Keith Ferrazzi and Tahl Raz
- *Who's Got Your Back: The Breakthrough Program to Build Deep, Trusting Relationships That Create Success—and Won't Let You Fail* by Keith Ferrazzi

- *How to Make People Like You in 90 Seconds or Less* by Nicholas Boothman
- *They Don't Teach Corporate in College, Third Edition* by Alexandra Levit
- *Love Is the Killer App: How to Win Business and Influence Friends* by Tim Sanders and Gene Stone
- *The World's Best Known Marketing Secret: Building Your Business with Word-of-Mouth Marketing* by Ivan R. Misner
- *The Tipping Point: How Little Things Can Make a Big Difference* by Malcolm Gladwell
- *Masters of Networking: Building Relationships for Your Pocketbook and Soul* by Ivan R. Misner and Don Morgan
- *Jeffrey Gitomer's Little Red Book of Selling: 12.5 Principles for Sales Greatness: How to Make Sales FOREVER* by Jeffrey Gitomer
- *Connected: The Surprising Power of Our Social Networks and How They Shape Our Lives* by Nicholas A. Christakis and James H. Fowler
- *The Fine Art of Small Talk: How to Start a Conversation, Keep It Going, Build Networking Skills—and Leave a Positive Impression!* by Debra Fine

Concluding Thoughts

he end of this book isn't the end of the process; rather, it's the beginning. In many ways, this book is like a personal fitness or meditation book. You can read about networking, but that won't make anything happen. You have to put what you learned into practice. You have to act on the ideas and use the tools you learned in this book. Until you do so, nothing will change. I once heard that, to an outsider, someone who has knowledge but doesn't use it looks exactly the same as an ignorant person. Let's make sure that no one mistakes you for an ignorant networker.

You don't have to start big to start. All it takes is one action. Email someone and invite them to coffee, register for an event, or sketch out your elevator speech on the back of a napkin. You can't build a network of contacts by sitting in your office or on your couch. Get out there and start shaking hands.

Here are a few final reminders for you as you build your network for the 21st century:

1. Set the vision. See your business and career thrive as you connect with others and help them build their businesses. Picture what it looks like to pass referrals to others and to receive new business opportunities in return. Picture what it

looks like to have these high-quality relationships. Visualize your success.

2. Invest the time. Once you've taken action, don't expect immediate returns on your effort. If it happens, that's great; but understand that you need to cultivate your network and spend the energy and effort up front. The benefits will come. Like a farmer, you have to nurture the seeds you plant over time so they'll bear fruit.

3. Help others. Every great networker knows their success comes by helping other people become successful. If you think networking is all about what's in it for you, you will struggle. It's networking karma. The more you reach out and support others, the more they will help your business blossom.

When I was growing up, my chores would often go undone. I was a pretty typical kid. My dad would walk into my room, and with a tone that is familiar to exasperated parents everywhere, he'd ask if I was waiting for a "Golden Invitation" to take out the garbage. Well, I'm leaving you with your Golden Invitation to the world of the successful networker. I invite you to act. I invite you to take the information you've learned and make it your own. I invite you to act on your vision and build the network that will make your professional dreams a reality.

I'll see you there!

The RockStars in My Life

've read hundreds of books and, therefore, hundreds of acknowledgement pages, but I didn't really understand how important these acknowledgments were until I wrote my own book and found out how much work is involved.

Now I understand why authors usually thank their editors first. From the beginning of our work together, Nancy Baumann balanced encouragement and praise with pages and pages of notes. She pointed out all of my glaring mistakes and gaps in the nicest way possible. And I'm lucky to have found an editor whose most common mantra is, "D., I want to hear more of YOU in this book."

I've met and networked with thousands of professionals in the last ten years, and I have to thank them all. It sounds corny, but whether it was a 30-second conversation by the appetizers or a quick introduction that blossomed into an ongoing friendship, I am truly grateful. Without your willingness and openness, my efforts at networking would have stalled from the beginning. And let's face it; all of my good ideas on networking—and business—are an amalgamation of best practices I learned from you along the way. Thank you!

My early mentors, teammates, and teachers at Cutco Cutlery have proven invaluable again and again in my career. Adam Stock, Marty Domitrovich, Mike Muriel, Danny Lewis, Jeff Bry, Joe Fingerhut,

Demian Scopp, Matt Long, Michelle Zeyda, and Luke Wojcik have all made an important imprint on my professional and personal life. And thank you to all of the other blade-slingers I haven't mentioned by name.

The team at Ajax Workforce Marketing helped me refine my thoughts on online networking and gave me the opportunity to be in the middle of the social media whirlwind. Jason Seiden's ideas on how technology impacts relationships gave me a lot of food for thought. Vince Gatti, Ben Prawer, Lisa Cervenka, Meaghan Edelstein, and Mary Toomey were also great conference companions—which was good because we went to more than one!

My first business coach, Fi Mazanke, was the person who showed me how to meld the yin and yang of intellectual pursuit with emotion and compassion. I am a better networker and businessperson because of it, and my career path was influenced in no small part by our work together.

For feedback, inspiration, and a sympathetic ear, I would be remiss to leave out Chrissie, Colette, Rob, Brian, Amy, and all of the other amazing people I've had a chance to surround myself with. Writing books can be lonely—it's always good to have someone on the other end of the phone when you need a break.

My family was my first network, and I got to test out my rela-tionship-building skills with my siblings: Anna, Laura, Danny, and Tommy. And my parents, to whom I dedicate this book, really are the best networkers I know. My siblings and I would often get impatient because we couldn't go anywhere without them running into someone they knew. They never read a book on how to be good networkers, they just lived it. Others responded to them because of who they are as people, and I learned the power of generosity, hard work, and loyalty from them. Pretty lucky for me!

And when you do your best writing early in the morning, and your significant other isn't a morning person—well, there can be a few disagreements over the alarm clock. Besides that, Helen has been my cheerleader, editor, sounding board, complaint hotline, biggest fan, and smoothie maker. From the day I said that I was going to write this book, she's been on board. Thank you for everything, my demanding flower.

D avid J.P. Fisher lives in Evanston, Illinois, next to a beautiful cemetery, which acts as a reminder every morning to not take life for granted. He is an entrepreneur, coach, salesman, writer, meditator, marketer, musician, son, friend, brother, slam poet, clairvoyant, comedian, salsa dancer, lover of life, teller of bad jokes, yoga enthusiast, and an average cook—as long as it's pancakes or hummus.

Known as D. Fish to everyone (except his mom), he is a sought-after speaker, author, and business coach. His passion for growth and development has allowed him to influence thousands of others during his professional career. As the current president of RockStar Consulting, he helps individuals become RockStars both offline and online by building their networking, sales, and entrepreneurial skills.

Want access to more resources to improve your networking skills? Stay connected with D. and what he's talking about in networking, entrepreneurship, and sales by visiting www.iamdfish.com.

Made in the USA
Lexington, KY
15 October 2015